"Karen Swallow Prior offers wisdom, experience, and horse sense not just to students preparing for the lives ahead of them but to adults who find themselves floundering. Calling, avocation, vocation, hobby, job, career, passion—Prior dissects each of these terms and matches them to both true and false ideas. *You Have a Calling* deftly identifies the lies that distort our sense of what we are meant to accomplish in life and outlines a better way forward."

—**Susan Wise Bauer**, author of *History of the Ancient World* and *The Well-Educated Mind*

"With her usual wisdom and clarity, Karen Swallow Prior dives deep into something that we all wrestle with: our place in the world and the work we've been given to do. I heartily commend this book, not only because Prior articulated many things I've felt to be true but have lacked the words for—but also because she challenged some of my assumptions and gently led me to a deeper understanding of my own calling. I closed this book with a renewed sense of purpose."

—**Andrew Peterson**, singer, songwriter, and author

"Karen Swallow Prior has gifted us a masterful exploration of what it truly means to be called. In *You Have a Calling*, she expertly weaves together theology, literature, and cultural wisdom, illuminating how our life's purpose is found not merely in what we do but profoundly in who we are becoming. Prior invites readers to embrace callings that transcend occupation, anchoring life's meaning firmly in the pursuit of the true, the good, and the beautiful. Richly nuanced, deeply reflective, and eloquently written, this book challenges contemporary misconceptions of vocation and reminds us that the highest calling is to live authentically before God, wherever we find ourselves. A profoundly refreshing read that every Christian—and especially young adults navigating life's big questions—ought to pick up and savor."

—**Anthony B. Bradley**, distinguished research fellow, The Acton Institute; research professor, Kuyper College

YOU
HAVE
A CALLING

YOU HAVE A CALLING

Finding Your Vocation in the
TRUE, GOOD, and BEAUTIFUL

KAREN SWALLOW PRIOR

BrazosPress
a division of Baker Publishing Group
Grand Rapids, Michigan

© 2025 by Karen Swallow Prior

Published by Brazos Press
a division of Baker Publishing Group
Grand Rapids, Michigan
BrazosPress.com

Printed in the United States of America

All rights reserved. No part of this publication may be reproduced, stored in a retrieval system, or transmitted in any form or by any means—for example, electronic, photocopy, recording—without the prior written permission of the publisher. The only exception is brief quotations in printed reviews.

Library of Congress Cataloging-in-Publication Data
Names: Prior, Karen Swallow, author.
Title: You have a calling : finding your vocation in the true, good, and beautiful / Karen Swallow Prior.
Description: Grand Rapids, Michigan : Brazos Press, a division of Baker Publishing Group, [2025]
Identifiers: LCCN 2024052019 | ISBN 9781587436659 (cloth) | ISBN 9781493450329 (ebook)
Subjects: LCSH: Vocation—Christianity. | Christian life.
Classification: LCC BV4740 .P76 2025 | DDC 248.4—dc23/eng/20250117
LC record available at https://lccn.loc.gov/2024052019

Scripture quotations taken from the Holy Bible, New International Version®, NIV®. Copyright © 1973, 1978, 1984, 2011 by Biblica, Inc.® Used by permission of Zondervan. All rights reserved worldwide. www.zondervan.com. The "NIV" and "New International Version" are trademarks registered in the United States Patent and Trademark Office by Biblica, Inc.®

Cover painting of *Reaper in a Flowery Meadow* by Frank Buchser, 1887
Cover design by Paula Gibson

Baker Publishing Group publications use paper produced from sustainable forestry practices and postconsumer waste whenever possible.

25 26 27 28 29 30 31   7 6 5 4 3 2 1

In memory of Shirley Ann Swallow (1936–2024),
who taught me what it means to be called

Contents

Questions	Work	Passion
1	**4**	**23**

Definitions	Calling	The Transcendentals
51	**55**	**83**

The True	The Good	The Beautiful
88	**104**	**116**

Acknowledgments	Notes
137	**139**

Questions

You have a calling.

In fact, you have more than one calling. Indeed, you will have various callings over the course of your lifetime. You may have callings now you don't even realize are callings. And you may have a calling or two that are yet to come.

But how do you know what your calling is? How can you be sure of it when it comes? And how do you know when a calling ends?

Not everyone will have the same answer to those questions. And the answers aren't always obvious or clear (although they can be blessedly so from time to time).

Sometimes the best way to answer hard questions is to ask good ones.

What if your calling isn't what you get paid to do?
What if it is?

What if your calling isn't something you feel passionate about every day—or even most days?

What if your calling doesn't bring you public fame or wide acclaim or much recognition at all? What if your calling is something no one sees?

What if your calling didn't come roaring into your ears like thunder rolling down from the mountains, so loud it was impossible to ignore? What if instead it hovered about like a pestering fly with a low, intermittent hum? What if you still can't quite hear that call?

What if your calling takes different forms over the course of your life, changing in shape, color, and size in the way an oak slowly grows from sapling to mighty timber, slipping each season from gold to green to brown to bare—all while remaining true as an oak?

What if a calling is something you can hear and answer only as you journey through life?

What if your calling is not an activity but a place? A town, a city, a farm, a country?

What if a calling isn't just about *what* you do but *how* you do it?

What if it isn't just about *doing* a certain thing but also about *being* a certain way?

Questions

I ought to say up front that this book is not going to tell you *what* your calling is. But I hope it will help show you *how* to discover and fulfill the various callings that unfold throughout your life.

Jesus said, "I am the way and the truth and the life" (John 14:6).

A way is a manner of going. It is the form our lives take on this worldly journey. The Christian is called to follow the way of Jesus. In Jesus is all truth, and he is truth. The answers to all our questions can be seen only by his light. And in him is all the goodness this life has to offer. In him alone is the good life. And the way of Jesus is beautiful.[1]

Jesus is the true, the good, and the beautiful.

As creatures made in the image of God, we are each called to pursue truth, goodness, and beauty in all of life.

Only in doing this can you discern and then follow your particular vocation, that particular work God created *you* to do.

And since we all must work—do good works, within our calling, around it, and alongside it—with work we will begin.

Work

Work has a bad reputation. This reputation is largely undeserved.

I'm thinking of bumper sticker sayings like, "A bad day of fishing is better than a good day at work" (which I know my husband agrees with!). Or "Find a job you love, and you will never have to work a day in your life." (The internet tells me this saying was originally stated by either Confucius or Mark Twain, who, along with C. S. Lewis, are the most commonly misattributed sources of popular quotes.)

These and other such sayings are rooted in an underlying assumption that work is bad. Or at least unpleasant and to be avoided. Certainly, much work can be hard, whether it be paid work or simply the work required to accomplish anything difficult that we set out to achieve.

Consider, though, how many ways we use the word "work" and the different contexts and connotations these uses of the word invoke. Artists create "works of art." A celebrity "works the crowd." When we exercise, we "work out." A knob on the radio has to be "worked a bit" to get the right channel. (Yes, I still have and use such a radio.) Recipes call for certain ingredients to be "worked in."[1] A conflict is "worked through." A lunch date is something we "work into" our overly scheduled calendars. Our salvation, St. Paul says, must be "worked out" in fear and trembling (Phil. 2:12).

All of these meanings suggest effort or exertion. And truly, as much as most of us would prefer a little less hustle and hurry in our lives, can you imagine a life without effort or exertion? It is as impossible as it is unimaginable. Would you even want such a life?

Even in the garden of Eden, work was part of life. In fact, God himself *worked* in forming creation, and he continues to work in ordering and sustaining it, remaining involved in the world he made and in the lives of those who bear his image. God was the first worker!

In *Garden City*, John Mark Comer contrasts this God of the Hebrew Scriptures with the gods described in other ancient literature. Those gods despised work. Humans were made essentially to serve as slave labor for these wicked deities.[2] But the God of Genesis—a creator, an artist, and a maker—took delight in his work. In making man and woman in his image, God bestowed on them—on all of us—the honor and responsibility of being his cocreators and partners, Comer says, in ruling over the earth. Not only that, but because we were made in his likeness, human beings are the visible representation in the world of the invisible God.[3] We are called to *present* God in and to the world.

This is the first calling of every human being: to bear witness to the God who created the world. We are all called to this work. God's original design for humanity remains even today. Everything we do re-presents God, whether ill or well.

I love the way John Milton in *Paradise Lost* imagines the work Adam and Eve did in Eden before the fall. Now, some of Milton's theology (not to mention his anthropology) is questionable, but his theology of work displayed in this poem is beautiful. In writing an epic poem that portrays humanity's expulsion from the garden, Milton imaginatively expands the spare details provided in just a few chapters of Genesis into an entire volume (twelve books of blank verse). Milton's description of Adam and Eve in Eden reminds us that work, according to the biblical narrative, was not a result of the fall but part of paradise itself.

But work done in a context of abundance (which is how Milton portrays the pre-fallen garden) differs from the labor required within a place of scarcity. Thus, in one passage, Adam describes the work he and Eve are about to do as "our delightful task / To prune these growing plants, and tend these flowers."[4] Later, Eve describes their efforts in even more detail:

> Adam, well may we labour still to dress
> This garden, still to tend plant, herb, and flower,
> Our pleasant task enjoined; but, till more hands
> Aid us, the work under our labour grows,
> Luxurious by restraint; what we by day
> Lop overgrown, or prune, or prop, or bind,

> One night or two with wanton growth derides
> Tending to wild . . .[5]

In such verdant environs as Eden, the first humans work not to procure but to prune, not to eke out but to contain—to dress, tend, lop, prune, prop, and bind the "wanton growth" of flowers, fruit, and foliage. Once humanity falls into sin, the curse laid upon them is not labor itself but labor accompanied by pain, whether the pangs of birth or those of thorns and thistles.

When I first moved to the near-tropical paradise of Virginia some years ago, I gained an entirely new perspective about the curse wrought by weeds. In Virginia, we have all the usual varieties of smaller vegetative pests—dandelions, buttercups, and crabgrass—harmless, even cute. (I do tend to let buttercups run wild!) But the weeds here include hardy, sometimes gargantuan vines and stalks that will grow as tall as trees and as thick as your wrist in one season if left unchecked. (Have you ever heard of pokeweed? If not, you are blessed indeed.) My gardening work consists primarily of pulling out (or sawing down!) the plants I don't want to grow and less tending of the plants I do want to grow.

Before embarking on my gardening-as-weeding adventures, I certainly understood the effects of sin on the world and our lives. But learning how quickly and vigorously strong weeds choke out tender beauties offered an object lesson like I never had before. The natural world visibly and tangibly displays the supernatural realities that surround us. This phenomenon includes the way work in the fallen world is encumbered with toil and strife.

The thorns, thistles, and labor pains that accompany our work today can take any number of forms. And while too much of a good thing can present its own problems, I think most would agree that scarcity—scarcity of work, opportunities, invitations, clients, money, time—is a weed that often chokes the joy and peace out of life. Sometimes that scarcity is real, very real. But other times it is our *fear* of scarcity—fear that money, opportunities, relationships, or capacity will be lacking—that drives our decisions, when we should be making choices based on our true calling rather than the fear of missing out.

God calls us to a life of abundance, not scarcity. God's economy is based on plenitude. If we believe that, accept it, see it, and own it, how different our decisions (and emotional states) might be.

Yet there are blessings even amid scarcity. They are just harder to recognize. Robert Hayden's poem "Those Winter Sundays" perfectly captures this. The speaker in the poem, a grown man, looks back on the work—and love—offered during his childhood by his father, a laborer during the week, who rose early on Sundays ("too" because he had to rise early the other days of the week as well) to warm the house and polish his son's boots. This calling was an "austere," lonesome, and difficult office for the father, whose sacrifice the son didn't recognize until long after:

> Sundays too my father got up early
> and put his clothes on in the blueblack cold,

> then with cracked hands that ached
> from labor in the weekday weather made
> banked fires blaze. No one ever thanked him.
>
> I'd wake and hear the cold splintering, breaking.
> When the rooms were warm, he'd call,
> and slowly I would rise and dress,
> fearing the chronic angers of that house,
>
> Speaking indifferently to him,
> who had driven out the cold
> and polished my good shoes as well.
> What did I know, what did I know
> of love's austere and lonely offices?[6]

Much has been said in recent years about the "crisis of manhood," particularly for men who are coming of age within a rapidly changing world in which work, roles, and family relationships are shifting underfoot like quicksand. In their search for significance, some young men (and women too) have turned increasingly to internet stars, celebrity gurus, famous new converts to Christianity, and the like as role models and inspiration. Most of the "work" by such people will not last, however. Hayden's poem offers a contrasting picture of the kind of work—often austere, lonely, and thankless—that will bear fruit for generations to come.

There will always be work to do. God works. He made us as creatures designed to join him in his work here on earth.

As Ben Witherington notes in *Work: A Kingdom Perspective on Labor*, there will also be work to do in the new heaven and the new earth, just as there was in that first paradise. The prophet Isaiah says some of that future work will entail beating swords into plowshares and spears into pruning hooks (Isa. 2:4), as well as building houses and planting vineyards (Isa. 65:21).[7]

Witherington opens his book by quoting the beginning of a poem by Emily Dickinson in which she contemplates the work and the workers that might be part of the afterlife. Here is the poem in its entirety:

> What is—"Paradise"—
> Who live there—
> Are they "Farmers"—
> Do they "hoe"—
> Do they know that this is "Amherst"—
> And that I—am coming—too—
>
> Do they wear "new shoes"—in "Eden"—
> Is it always pleasant—there—
> Won't they scold us—when we're homesick—
> Or tell God—how cross we are—
>
> You are sure there's such a person
> As "a Father"—in the sky—
> So if I get lost—there—ever—
> Or do what the Nurse calls "die"—
> I shan't walk the "Jasper"—barefoot—
> Ransomed folks—won't laugh at me—
> Maybe—"Eden" a'n't so lonesome
> As New England used to be![8]

Dickinson wonders if the inhabitants of heaven will be workers doing the kind of work they did on earth: "farmers" who "hoe." Her use of quotation marks with various words throughout the poem suggests the emblematic nature of these images. If this world ("New England") is a picture of the next world, then the death that will bring her to the new Eden will be a kind of work to "do." Someone in heaven will be making shoes. Because of their work, she won't have to walk barefoot on the jeweled streets of the new Jerusalem: jasper is one of the precious stones mentioned in the new heavenly city described in Revelation 21. A city, of course, is a place made by human work—although even nature and gardens require work to make the country hospitable and beautiful to human creatures, as Adam and Eve well knew.

The biblical narrative begins in a garden and ends in a city. Christians sometimes get caught up in debates about which of these settings in this life is ideal and which is the more important place to serve people and build God's kingdom. These are the wrong questions. Some are called to the city, some are called to the country, and some to the places in between. The Bible makes clear that there is work—good work—to do everywhere.

Proverbs 31 paints another beautiful picture of work. While this passage is too-commonly characterized as portraying a certain kind of woman, the verses are better read as a description of the way any virtuous person works. The passage celebrates good work done well.[9] The woman described is the personification of wisdom, which is a central theme throughout the book of Proverbs. She is, as Old Testament scholar Dominick Hernández puts it, "the exemplar of wisdom for all people."[10]

The work of Wisdom described in Proverbs 31 is not only varied but also integrated into a holistic and well-rounded life. There is no division between public and private or between sacred and secular. Wisdom's work takes place in the marketplace and in the home. Her work blesses the community and her family alike. Most importantly, she serves the Lord in it all. Her good work will bring her praise at the city gate. This description is one all of us should aspire to in pursuing the good, true, and beautiful in our work.

The way in which Proverbs 31 integrates work done in public and private, as well as work done for the community and the family, is worth particular attention, for the passage portrays it all as worship. Dorothy Sayers addresses this all-encompassing vision of labor in her iconic essay "Why Work?" She writes there, "It is the business of the Church to recognize that the secular vocation, as such, is sacred." The church, Sayers argues, ought not concede to the wrongheaded, worldly idea that one's life "is divided into the time he spends on his work and the time he spends in serving God. He must be able to serve God in his work, and the work itself must be accepted and respected as the medium of divine creation."[11]

This evocative turn of phrase deserves more attention. Work is "the medium of divine creation." This means that God creates through our work. (Obviously, Sayers is not saying that this is the only way God creates but that this is just one way he creates.) When was the last time you thought of your work as the medium—the paint, the film, the ink, the lead, the stage, the viola, the field, the boardroom, the Zoom call, the dough, the sewing machine, the knitting needles, the laptop—for God's creative activity? When was the last time you thought of yourself as an artist even in the most mundane or ordinary daily work? You are his hands and feet. He works through you. He creates through you. "That is our calling: co-creation," writes Madeleine L'Engle. "Every single one of us, without exception, is called to co-create with God."[12]

Last summer, when my mother was dying but we didn't yet realize it, my friend Melissa stopped by to visit and bring my father tomatoes from her garden. My father loves a good tomato. He insists you cannot find a good one in the grocery store. As we were chatting, the subject of this book came up, and Melissa talked about all the things people do in pursuit of their callings. "And some people," my father said quietly, "grow tomatoes." This, too, is co-creation.

Co-creation is perhaps the most fruitful reading of Lady Wisdom in Proverbs 31. Through her works the Lord's work is done. She is, like the church itself, Christ's bodily presence in the world, making him known through her wise, gracious, good work.

In "The Elixir," seventeenth-century English poet-priest George Herbert describes work done for God as the secret formula that gives meaning to all our work. An elixir was once thought to be a magical ingredient by which alchemists could turn base metal into gold. Such a potion does not exist, of course. But Herbert takes that mythical idea and applies it to the transformation that can happen even with our meanest work when it is done "for Thy sake":

You Have a Calling

Teach me, my God and King,
    In all things Thee to see,
And what I do in anything
    To do it as for Thee.

    Not rudely, as a beast,
        To run into an action;
But still to make Thee prepossest,
    And give it his perfection.

    A man that looks on glass,
        On it may stay his eye;
Or if he pleaseth, through it pass,
    And then the heav'n espy.

    All may of Thee partake:
        Nothing can be so mean,
Which with his tincture—"for Thy sake"—
    Will not grow bright and clean.

    A servant with this clause
        Makes drudgery divine:
Who sweeps a room as for Thy laws,
    Makes that and th' action fine.

    This is the famous stone
        That turneth all to gold;
For that which God doth touch and own
    Cannot for less be told.[13]

Devoting our work to God's purposes is the "famous stone" that turns it all to gold. Rather than looking *at* our work, we can look *through* it (as we look through a glass window) in order to see what God is doing through us for his kingdom.

But notice that the poem begins by imploring God, "Teach me." Seeing our work in this way does not come naturally or easily. But when we learn to see through our labor to see more of him, he "makes drudgery divine." Even the work of sweeping a room becomes "fine."

Human beings will always have work. It is part of the human condition. Work itself is a good that is part of God's original design and therefore contributes to human flourishing. And while work and calling do overlap at times, they are not the same (as I will keep repeating throughout these pages). Perhaps recognizing how they are different can help us appreciate what each is and what role each has in our individual lives and in our communal life together.

We were created to work—just as our Creator works—and that work will be part of the new heaven and the new earth. Understanding that can give us the perspective that work will never end—not because it's bad but because it's good.

Even so, the nature, meaning, and role of work shift due to the changes that take place within larger social frameworks—even from one generation to the next. Moreover, there are infinite kinds of good work we might do.

Having many possibilities is liberating. But as anyone who has experienced the fear of missing out or analysis paralysis knows, it can be crippling too. Life in the modern world is characterized by, among other things, an increased sense of individual agency and responsibility for our lives compared to previous times. This increased sense of responsibility makes our decisions around work more fraught and anxious in a way our ancestors, who had few or no choices, did not experience. The medieval person born into a peasant family and their peer born into royalty knew their callings. Most of us today don't, at least not at first. Perhaps not ever.

The Protestant work ethic that in many ways brought about this modern condition—in which we believe we bear the ultimate responsibility for our work and, therefore, for the outcome of our lives—sought to erase the false distinction between secular and sacred vocations. As Sayers explains in the passage above, this is a good and right understanding. Paradoxically, however, this same idea has contributed to the erasure of the concept of vocation altogether.

The Reformation's emphasis on the significance of all types of work created new social and economic opportunities for work. What resulted were conditions in which one's labor could generate economic benefits for oneself, not only one's lords and rulers. Work undertaken for self-interest naturally leads to motivation to work harder and better, a phenomenon that in great part defines the modern condition and the rise of the modern individual. Work in such cultural circumstances becomes not merely a necessary calling based on the circumstances of one's birth but also an opportunity for advancement and improvement.

Daniel Defoe's 1722 novel *Moll Flanders* illustrates the changing nature of work in the modern age.[14] This fictional story is presented as a true memoir of a woman who, born in Newgate prison to a convict, scrambles her way through life via her own pluck and resourcefulness. The story centers on the various kinds of work Moll does (much of it illegal) in order to survive and ultimately thrive. She reaches the end of her life wealthy and penitent, having employed herself along the way as servant, mistress, swindler, and thief. Defoe shows how Moll understands herself and the conditions of her life in the language she uses to describe her work. She softens the criminal aspects of her career by using euphemistic language. She calls her forays out onto the city streets to steal "adventures," "excursions," or taking "a walk." She describes skills in robbery as an "art," a "craft," and the "trade," and she calls her fellow thieves "artists."[15]

Now, Defoe is making a great deal of social (and religious) commentary in this story, much of which exceeds my purposes here. But what we can see happening through Moll's narrative, one in which she pulls herself up by her own (as well as others') bootstraps, is that work becomes connected to personal, social, and economic improvement rather than being strictly an answer to a vocational call. (Interestingly, there is a moment in the story when Moll hears the audible call of one of her several [serial] husbands calling for her to return to him, and she does.) Defoe, it is relevant to note, was a Puritan (specifically, a Presbyterian) who held a number of political and business positions as he struggled throughout his life (sometimes unsuccessfully) to keep himself out of debtors' prison. Defoe's life, along with his character, demonstrates the new and tremendous pressure and anxiety felt by the modern person who is not lucky enough to be born into position and wealth to make something of themselves. The struggle is real. Os Guinness warns in his classic book *The Call* that a culture unmoored from a sense of calling and built on unrestrained capitalism, like the one Defoe portrays in *Moll Flanders*, is destined toward hedonism. Such a world reduces work to merely a means of gaining more money and more possessions on the terms of the free market.[16]

In reading literature like this, we can observe the concept of vocation changing in real time, slowly being replaced by the modern notion of upward mobility and the desire for its newly attainable economic advantage. The idea of having a calling slowly evolved from holding a spiritual office (whether in the church or family) into making a living and having worldly success. *Moll Flanders* reflects Guinness's observation that over the course of the modern age the "original demand that each Christian should have a calling was boiled down to the demand that each citizen should have a job," and eventually work itself "was made sacred."[17]

Sacralizing work, however, desacralized the sense of the Caller and thus calling. Now, like Moll, we have a long menu of terms we use to refer to work: *job, career, gig, employment, position, post, appointment,* and *occupation*, to name a few. Now, instead of *calling*, late modernity hands us *options, choices, opportunities, advancements, promotions, demotions, lateral moves*—and gives us constant change over stability.

Meanwhile, the word "vocation," as Guinness points out, is often assigned to the categories of jobs taken by workers who undergo "vocational training" rather than go to college, the kind of work disdained by the socially elite and highly educated.[18] Looking down on any kind of "good work" (a favorite phrase of my father), however, reflects a diminished or distorted view of vocation. A robust view of vocation values the gifts and skills that vary from person to person and celebrates the good use of those gifts and skills.

This impoverished view of vocation, as portrayed above in large sweeps, has occurred over several centuries. But within narrower pockets of time—over the span of each succeeding generation in recent decades—we can see smaller shifts that feel terribly dramatic from one generation to another.

Members of the Silent Generation (born between 1928 and 1945) strived to work at one job or company for their entire career, earning a dependable salary, health insurance, a pension, and other benefits. Baby boomers and Gen Xers (that's me) could hope for the same but might expect to move around in order to move up. But for millennials and those following them, that kind of continuity and certainty barely exists. In years past, I remember having to explain to some of my students looking for their first postgraduation jobs that "full-time" refers not just to a certain number of hours worked per week but also to the benefits that usually (or used to) come with such a position. But those conversations occurred in a context in which that option was more available. Now, just a few years later, we live in what is often called the gig economy, one in which more and more people (including me) are cobbling together various combinations of temporary and part-time jobs in order to make a living.

Within each of these contexts, work itself takes on a different character. Work shifted from being a means of supporting oneself and one's family to being not only that but also a vehicle of greater personal fulfillment and eventually a means for fulfilling one's passion (as we'll consider at length in the next chapter). All this to say that each generation encounters its own challenges in discerning one's calling, if that is even part of the equation (again, understanding that work and calling are not the same).

The autoworker of the past who clocked in daily and collected a weekly paycheck may have found his primary calling not in his work but in providing for his family, in having camaraderie with coworkers with whom he could share a beer in the neighborhood bar after work, and in simply being a part of his community. But in subsequent generations, particularly for those who invested significant time and money into going to college in order to obtain career success, finding one's primary calling in work has become a general expectation.

In recent years, however, as a result of spiraling tuition and cost of living, many college graduates have found such an expectation difficult, if not impossible, to fulfill. The more one's employment is linked to one's calling, the more likely it is that jobs that don't meet that criterion will be viewed as stepping stones to the ideal job, and the more likely it is that people will move jobs over the course of their working lives. As Guinness points out, the "increase in choice and change" that characterizes modern life "leads to a decrease in commitment and continuity."[19] There are certainly pros and cons for successive jobs of shorter duration, but as we'll examine in more detail in the next chapter, sometimes the benefits of staying in one job for a long time are overlooked. Certainly, commitment goes two ways, and employers are often at fault for not being committed to their employees, which is a greater problem in the long run. Nevertheless, there is wisdom in considering the benefits that we as individuals can give and receive through our own commitment to and continuity in our work.

The bigger point, however, is simply that work has not always looked the same or meant the same thing from generation to generation, a fact that can be easy to miss from within one's own particular circumstance.

While we must work—just as human beings in all times and places have had to do—we in the modern age possess, along with more choices than our forebears generally had, a greater sense of burden and responsibility in making those choices. Within such a context, a job isn't just a source of income but can be seen as a way to fulfill a greater purpose.

A general greater purpose, however, may not be (or at least may not feel like) *your own* greater purpose. Sometimes a person steps into a role not because it is the role they have long dreamed of but simply because they are particularly equipped and able to fill a particular need at a particular time. Finding work that aligns with our passions, desires, and gifts is, of course, ideal. It just doesn't always happen, and that is okay. It doesn't mean there is something wrong with you. Somehow we've gotten to a place in our world where people think there is something lacking in them when that alignment doesn't happen or doesn't happen right away. I always get comfort and a chuckle when I see the "Venn diagram of my life" meme. It shows three circles labeled "Things I like to do," "Things I'm good at," and "Things that make money." Only the first two slightly overlap. There is no overlap with "Things that make money." This meme, like so many others, exists to remind us that we are not alone.

Calling transcends all these categories. Ultimately, we can trust that when we are called, the call will—eventually—come through. Sometimes it might require a few tries to make the connection. Sometimes the call gets dropped. Sometimes someone gets a wrong number. But if we keep working at it, the call will come.

Passion

"Follow your passion."

This little proverb is repeated so often—whether expressed verbatim or more metaphorically or imaginatively through art—that it's easy to mistake its counsel for a universal, timeless, self-evident truth.

It's not.

As life advice, this idea is a fairly novel concept, reaching axiomatic status only late in the twentieth century. If you plug the phrase "follow your passion" or "pursue your passion" into Google's Ngram Viewer (a database of print sources dated between the years 1500 and 2019), you will find that both of these phrases were nearly nonexistent until the 1990s—at which point they suddenly appear on the graph and shoot straight up like a tower.

The advice is not self-evident either. In fact, Cal Newport, the Georgetown computer science professor known for his research on productive work, calls it "dangerous advice."[1] I've never put it so starkly as that, but Newport's stance—backed up by ample research—is a view I've held for years, albeit based on gut instinct and anecdotal evidence I gained over decades of teaching young people raised with this idea. My suspicion about this folk advice is also rooted in my observations about how idealism and unrealistic expectations not only lead to disappointment and disillusionment but also can rob us of the joy to be found in ordinary, everyday life. Newport's research shows that we become more passionate about what we become good at—and being good at something takes time, experience, and experimentation. In support of his argument, Newport cites an interesting study from a survey of college administrative assistants. This occupation was chosen for the study because it's not an occupation most people aspire to or dream about early in life. It's not work most people would initially pursue out of passion. Guess what? The survey found that the administrative assistants most likely to see their work as a calling (rather than just a job or a stepping stone) were those who had the most experience in the role.[2] As another researcher summarizes the point, "When your passion is based on your skills, losing your job can't even take that away. Your passion will follow you so long as you put in the work."[3] In other words, you really do have to work it.

Not only might passion follow experience, but that experience and the competence that comes with it can benefit others. On this point, Newport's research connects well with an observation my husband has made for years in his role as a public school teacher. He entered teaching in midlife as a second career, although his calling has long been the same (building and creating). He learned construction from his father, who

Passion

was a contractor. For years, my husband was also a contractor, but he then moved into teaching those skills to others. Being a vocational teacher (*ahem*, see the observation above about the use of that term), he still does a lot of hands-on work himself. He is finishing up twenty years in his role as a teacher at one school. Many of his fellow teachers there have had even longer tenures. Something my husband has noticed over these years is the impact made on the long-term staff when administrators come and go as if through a revolving door. Every new administrator arrives with new ideas and big plans (which are usually piled on top of the new ideas and big plans implemented by the previous administrators). There's a constant sense of starting over and breaking in as a result. "No one stays," my husband often observes. As a result, no one gains the time in one place and one community that brings the benefits and blessings that only such time spent over the long haul can bring.

Of course, that doesn't mean every person can do every single task well just because they work at it. Limitations and inabilities are built into being human. Each of us has weaknesses, just as each of us has strengths.

This fact brings me to another bit of false folk wisdom—that faulty refrain: "You can do anything!"

I vividly remember the first time a high school student told me she could do anything if she wanted to badly enough. We were in my office discussing her ongoing struggles in her classes, especially in math and science. Trying to encourage and guide her helpfully, I asked her what she wanted to pursue after high school. "I want to be an ob-gyn," she said. I gently pointed out the central role of math and science in this field. "My mother told me I can be anything," she countered confidently. I didn't know what to say in the moment. I didn't want to undermine her mother. Nor did I want to fail to advise the student wisely. In the end, her math and science grades never considerably improved, and this experience (and many that followed) shaped my views about the ways in which these unhelpful, feel-good sayings were setting up young people for near-certain disappointment. At the same time, such misdirection makes it even harder to find a true calling.

Over the ensuing years, in my role as a college professor, I held my students to high expectations, while at the same time helping them see the world more realistically than they tended to. Young people of all times tend toward idealism, of course. But the young people I taught were living in a new world in which social media was inundating them with image after image of shiny, happy people who seemingly became overnight successes at whatever they had set their hearts on when they were mere teens.

Often students would come to my office for advice. Sometimes the advice they were seeking centered on my life: they wanted to know how to be just like me, to do what I do. They knew I was a longtime professor who had earned a doctorate at a relatively young age, had risen through the academic ranks to become a full professor, and was becoming more widely published. But they weren't seeing what it had taken to get there.

When asked by aspiring writers, creatives, and future academics how to be like me, I would generally begin by saying, "Well, if you want to be like me, you won't publish your first book until you're forty-seven." Then I would pause while their twenty-one-year-old jaws dropped to the floor. This was not what they expected or wanted to hear. It took me a while to understand just how many messages to the contrary they were getting, and how often.

Looking back, I suppose I was sort of a dream squasher. I didn't mean to be. I just think dreams are more readily achieved by having realistic ones.

That conviction is how I ended up making fellow writer Sarah Sanderson determined to prove me wrong about her.

When she was still in the early throes of writing and publishing her first book, Sarah reached out in a social media group for advice from more seasoned writers. I responded by saying something along the lines of what I've told countless students (and others) over the years: just because you write something doesn't mean someone else will want to publish it. Lots of people, I've found, don't know that there is a substantial difference between writing and being published. Some want the status of being a published author without being necessarily committed to the craft of writing, and even more aspiring writers know little about how publishing works. I didn't know Sarah at that time, but I offered my usual point and then forgot all about the exchange.

Some time later, I received an email from a first-time author whose name I didn't recall, asking me to read and consider endorsing her book manuscript. (Like most writers, I get many such requests.) Something about the email and the subject matter of the book got my attention, and I glanced at the manuscript. Then I read it. And then I endorsed it. Enthusiastically.

Only later did Sarah tell me that she was the one I'd discouraged with my words about not expecting to get published. I didn't remember our earlier exchange, but I felt a little sheepish, so I asked her to remind me. She recalled what I described above and then offered the effect my words had on her:

> I felt chagrined, as if you'd failed to recognize that I was more special than the general unwashed mass of bad writers (though how could you have?), and as if I was supposed to just go ahead and conclude that this desire that I'd been lugging around for half my life was nothing more than a hobby. But . . . rather than taking it as a sign that I truly wasn't supposed to keep going on that path, I held your comment in my mind as a kind of foil, a yardstick against which I hoped to prove myself. "Karen Swallow Prior thinks I'm just a hobbyist," I often thought to myself. "I'm going to prove her wrong."[4]

And she did.

So perhaps my hard advice helped? Even if it ultimately did, I've learned since then (I hope) to try to be a bit gentler in my dream squashing.

I suppose young people (all people, of course, but we call it "youthful idealism" for a reason) have always struggled to temper expectations in this regard. But I also think some cultural shifts have made such idealism even more characteristic of these times. For example, those raised under helicopter parents (always hovering) or snowplow parents (always plowing away obstacles that might impede a child's wishes) will, not surprisingly, expect to accomplish what they desire at an accelerated rate with few challenges. Perhaps even more influential is a media-saturated society in which material goods and personal successes are spread out before us on an endless conveyor belt, tantalizing, tempting, mocking, displaying the outcomes but seldom the processes or means required to achieve them. Millennial entrepreneur and podcaster Kate Kennedy, for example, writes that she felt frustrated early in her career because she "fell for a lot of lofty inspirational stories" about career success, stories that seldom provided the background details of that front-facing success.[5] This has been a common experience for the generations that have grown up as digital natives.

You didn't have to grow up in this environment to be affected by it, however. The idea that we all must pursue our passion is in the air we breathe. It has affected us all.

But before we consider the wisdom of pursuing your passion, we need to know what passion is.

The way we use the word today, we tend to think of "passion" as an intense love or desire. And it certainly is. But there is more to the history of the word and its wider usage that is helpful to bring to our attention.

The original Latin root word from which the word "passion" comes means "suffering." That might seem odd at first, but consider other words that come from the same root: "patient" and "patience," for example. A patient staying in the hospital or receiving medical care is someone who is suffering. Likewise, any situation that requires us to exercise patience is a situation that causes some level of suffering. A person waiting patiently in line virtuously endures the suffering; an impatient person resists that suffering by blustering and stamping about. Within the context of romance, a passionate lover suffers from the intensity of burning desire. The starving artist is so committed to pursuing an inner passion that he would rather live in poverty than give up that pursuit. The phrases denoting Christ's crucifixion and the events leading up to it—"the passion of Christ" and "passion week"—refer to Christ's suffering through these events. He is also described in the Old Testament prophetically as the suffering servant (Isa. 52 and 53). This is why it can be said, "The martyr and the lover are the archetypes of passion."[6] This is the sense of suffering that comes with the word "passion" as we continue to use it today, a sense of suffering that is often romanticized.

With these examples, we can see that suffering isn't always merely something bad that happens to us but can be willingly endured for something greater. We might admire the work of great artists such as Vincent van Gogh or Ludwig van Beethoven, but most of us wouldn't want to *be* them given how much they suffered for their art. And few if any people suffer without causing further suffering to those around them.

All this might seem like a heavy way to begin thinking about the role that our passions play in our lives. We certainly don't think about the torment of Christ on the cross when thinking about the passion we have for photography, for example, or singing or cooking or traveling. But understanding that passion in its true sense entails suffering can help us distinguish between something that piques our curiosity or offers a mild, passing interest and those things that are burning drives or desires deep within.

The words "desire" and "passion" are not interchangeable. One way to distinguish between them is to think of passion as a more intense and ongoing form of desire.

Some desires and passions seem natural to us, coming completely unbidden or unasked for. But some desires are cultivated, emerging from surroundings and experiences. It's fascinating to think about where our passions and desires come from. I suspect the short answer is that they owe their existence, like so much in our lives, to a combination of nature and nurture.

One of my favorite and most formative illustrations of how God gives us our desires comes from Henry Blackaby's classic text, *Experiencing God*. Blackaby tells one memorable story as a way of explaining the meaning of Psalm 37:4, which says, "Take delight in the LORD, and he will give you the desires of your heart." It's not that God grants us our human desires apart from him, as though God were a kind of genie in a bottle. Rather, this psalm says that God will cultivate within us desires for the good things he has for us. To illustrate this,

Blackaby tells of a time when he gave his six-year-old son the very present the boy wanted—a blue Schwinn bicycle. The real story, however, was not the giving of the gift but the father cultivating in the child beforehand a desire for the gift he was intending for his son all along. So, *after* buying and hiding the bicycle in the garage, Blackaby built a desire in his son's heart for the bicycle by talking about and describing it until the boy began to long for it. Imagine the boy's delight upon receiving on his birthday his "heart's desire"—the very gift his father had wanted him to have.[7] Of course, this isn't a perfect analogy. But God does create each of us according to his plans and purposes. And he gives us desires to draw us toward his purposes.

Another way passion and desire differ is that passions tend to be out there flying high above the surface, waving enthusiastically at everyone. Desires often run deeper, more quietly, perhaps even hidden from ourselves. How often do we pursue one thing—a job, a membership, a designer bag—not because we want that thing but because we think having that thing will fulfill some deeper desire, such as the desire for belonging or acceptance?

As human beings, we desire many things, some of them needs, some just wants: food, sex, warmth, love, entertainment, an SUV, that cute sweater at Anthropologie. Some of these desires come from our basic existence as biological human beings, some come from the necessities of modern life, and some are cultivated (even artificially constructed) through marketing, peer groups, and whatever social or psychological feedback loop we find ourselves in. Some desires need not, nor ever will, reach the level of passion, while others will develop into passions.

But we live in a hyperbolic age. This is an age in which *everything* is *the best thing ever* (or *the worst thing ever*), an age in which we use the word "awesome" when we finally land on that mutually workable date for coffee between two overscheduled friends, leaving us no word with which to express something truly awesome—like, say, the glory of God. (I am not immune to this tendency! If you ask me what my favorite novel is or the one everyone should read, I will give you a list. They are all my "favorite"!)

Yet the truth is that we don't have to be passionate about everything—or even about many things. In fact, it is good and healthy to distinguish between degrees of desire and drive.

To be clear, passion can be good, as pursuing our passions can be good. Passion is like fuel. It is the energy that fuels us toward some purpose. Purpose is the *why*; passion is the *how*. Passion apart from purpose is just a can of gas. As with fuel, we can burn with too much passion, or passion can drive us in the wrong direction. Or we can pursue a passion for a good thing in ways that neglect other goods in our life, in the way that uncontained fuel can burn. Or we can feel like a failure because the passionate pursuit didn't turn out as planned. We can even feel we are somehow deficient because we lack a particular passion or haven't achieved a level of intensity we somehow imagine is necessary.

Especially within the contemporary world, there can be a lot of pressure to "find your passion" or to "have a passion for [fill in the blank]."

I think, for example, of a friend who felt something was wrong with her because she lacked intense passion. She tried for years to artificially stir up intense emotions about her faith, her work, and her interests. It turns out she's just an even-keeled, steady person. (We need more such people in the world!) Some people are more naturally driven and intense than others. While apathy and depression (which we find at the other extreme of passion) are neither desirable nor healthy, that doesn't mean that the person who is staid by disposition ought to artificially whip up intense feelings just to have a passion.

I think, too, of parents I've known over the years who shuffled their children from lesson to lesson, activity to activity, sport to sport, trying to get the kids passionately interested in something. The harder the parents tried, it seemed, the more overcome by boredom and listlessness these youngsters became. Of course, a life without interest, curiosity, or desire is no life at all. But not everyone is destined to be driven by an all-consuming passion. And sometimes a passion just takes a long time to germinate inside before it can grow strong enough and mature enough to introduce itself to you by name.

In sum, a passion or desire is not good or bad in and of itself. Like loyalty, the goodness of a desire depends on the goodness of its object. Furthermore, passions must be moderated in order to be virtuous and healthy. We can strive to temper our passions by the desires and demands of the rest of life's responsibilities and relationships.

Passion

While passions can be cultivated and grow, they can also wane over the course of our lives. This is why we should be careful about placing our identity in our passions.

I am passionate about animals in general. That has not changed. That is something that, I suspect, is core to who I am, though it has taken different forms and worked out in different ways in the various stages of my life and work. For most of my life, I was what is called a "horse person." My passion for horses forms some of my earliest memories from childhood. I read every horse book I could get my hands on, visited horse farms on family vacations, got my first horse when I was eleven, worked on horse farms during college and graduate school, and spent half of my moving allowance from my first real job to transport my horse to my new home several states away. But, after my last horse died at a ripe old age, things in my life had changed enough—and my passions along with them—that I decided that Desperado, my smart little Paso Fino, would be my last horse. I've been horseless now these last ten years. And you know what? I don't miss it at all, really. Horses are a lot of work. And that is especially what I don't miss.

But my dogs? That's another story. I am passionate about my Ruby and Eva. In fact, I have experienced only a few substantial and lasting traumas in my life. One of them was getting hit by a bus. Another was losing our Ruby for four days after she took off in the woods one time when she was a rascally young pup. Of those two, I can easily rank the trauma of losing Ruby and the prospect of never finding her as a deeper and longer-lasting trauma. Oh, how I suffered from love of her. And how grateful I am to God for bringing her back to us—whole, if not entirely unharmed. I think about it literally every day.

Passions begin inside of us but express themselves outside of us. The objective goodness of something is not measured by the depth or breadth of our passion for it. Passion is subjective, individual, and changing. ("Oh, Willoughby, Willoughby!" One cannot read these words of foolish Marianne Dashwood in Jane Austen's *Sense and Sensibility* and ever think of passion so naively again.[8]) More importantly, we can have more than one passion. "If you have two or three real passions, don't feel like you have to pick and choose between them," writes bestselling author and artist Austin Kleon. "Don't discard. Keep all your passions in your life."[9]

Recognizing all this can, I think, help us embrace our passions and, at the same time, help us hold them loosely with wonder and delight, not for the passions themselves but rather for how they can draw us toward the true, the good, and the beautiful things of the world.

As we've seen, passion covers a lot of ground, from the literal torture and death of Jesus to romantic feelings to intense interests such as a love of photography. Pursuing your passion can mean getting paid to do what you're interested in, but it can also simply mean investing time, devoting resources, and making sacrifices for something (or someone) you love.

Yet today the expression "Pursue your passion" is often interpreted or assumed to mean "Get paid to do what you love." Now, of course, there is nothing wrong—and much that can be blessed and right!—about getting paid to do what you love to do. (I'm grateful to be lucky enough to have experienced that very thing for much of my life.) On the other hand, we will be required to do many things over the course of our lives, most of which we aren't, in fact, passionate about—and many things we are but don't get paid for.

It's important to parse out the various meanings and assumptions of these words and phrases, because they can easily get funneled into narrow applications that distort our understanding and our expectations. I've had countless people tell me that hearing this message, "Pursue your passion," has made them feel like a failure for not being passionate about their jobs. Some have even said they have heard this advice so often that they've never stopped to think about the fact that many (if not most) people aren't passionate about what they do for a living—that it's just a living. (Notice that it's called "a living," not "living." There's a difference.)

It gets worse. Some people I know have been told that if they aren't pursuing their passion in their employment, they are not doing God's will. Now, it certainly is true that we must steward our passions and our opportunities to pursue those passions. Being born in a time and place in which that is possible is itself a gift of God's sovereign will that must be stewarded well. But imagine the vast majority of workers and providers across the planet, toiling day in and day out to eke out a living for themselves and for those dependent on them—imagine telling them they're out of God's will because they aren't *passionate* about their paid work.

The sports world is one place where we can be reminded of the goodness of being an amateur, someone who participates for the love of the game without being a paid professional. Many sports associations maintain rigid rules that divide the amateur from the professional. From ancient times into the twentieth century, the Olympic Games, for example, were strictly for amateurs—no professionals allowed!—but that changed over the past several decades for a number of reasons. Perhaps the greatest factor was televising the games: professional players simply attract more viewers. These rules can be muddied by financial interests and politics, but the long-standing distinction between amateur and professional is helpful to keep in mind.

At the distinction's core is the acknowledgment that some great passions can be pursued out of sheer love—indeed, the word "amateur" comes from a French word that means "love." In fact, 96 percent of the passions identified by people in one study had no relation to their work but were instead connected to hobbies and other interests.[10] By no means is anyone a failure or sinful merely because their day job is not their passion.

My friend Myndi Lawrence is a great lover of art, literature, and dance. She has spent the past couple of decades raising four children and helping out at their homeschool cooperative. In that role, Myndi has written, adapted, and produced plays for students to perform at the end of each school year.

Myndi doesn't get paid to do this. It's just something she contributes to the education of her children and the other members of their educational community. But here's the amazing thing: among all the people I know who love the performing arts, I don't know many (if any) who've had the opportunity to write and produce as many plays as Myndi has. She has been able to pursue her passion as a playwright and producer for the stage to an extent that others only dream of. Doing this has also led to opportunities for Myndi to cowrite and coproduce original works for a local dance studio. Yet it was only recently that Myndi came to see this work, which she does out of passion, as a true calling. And it is.

For the most part, and for most of us, merely having a desire or a passion inside us does not necessarily mean we will receive a call from outside that will fulfill that passion. Some people have a passion for *The Lord of the Rings*. (Actually, a lot of people do!) But only 0.00001 percent of people with that passion are going to get a call to be part of making a film or filling a role related to the series. And yet anyone can talk about it, tweet about it, join book clubs about it, and critique the film adaptations 'til the sun goes down! That's a passion, not a vocation.

As another example, I have a passion for running. I run almost every day and have done so for most of my life, ever since I failed to make the cheerleading team in junior high and joined the cross-country team instead. (They let anyone join cross-country.) But no one, and I mean no one, is calling me to run for them. If you've seen me run, that would be obvious (although I actually did pretty well on the team by my junior year of high school!). My purpose in running these days isn't to win a race or even to train for one. My passion to run is how I fulfill my need to live a balanced life—taking a break from the sedentary, indoor life of writing and reading to get outside and move my body while my brain rests.

We used to call these things we love to do for fun—things like Tolkien fan culture or running—"hobbies." That's a quaint word you don't hear very often anymore. A more technical word—one we also don't hear often anymore—is "avocation." While "vocation" describes one's work or job, "avocation" denotes what one pursues outside of work—simply out of love, out of passion. Originally, "avocation" meant a move away from one's calling or work. Notice that the assumption built into these categories is that what one does for money is not necessarily (or even likely to be) something one loves to do. The fact is that being paid to do what you love has, for most of human history, been the exception, not the rule.

Coffee lovers offer a simple illustration of how a passion can play out.

Some people are passionate about roasting, brewing, and serving excellent coffee and have turned that passion into paid work. Some people are passionate about drinking coffee and develop all sorts of knowledge and nuance about how they prefer it, which no one pays them to share or indulge in. Someone passionate about coffee (as I was from the age of twenty-two until about now) might experience that passion changing, even unwillingly, as they reach a certain age in which they can stomach half a cup of their beloved black coffee each day and no more! The point is that passions even for the same thing can take a different form for everyone, and those forms and the passions themselves can change over the course of our lives too. (And, by the way, a taste for coffee is, for most people, cultivated rather than natural, pointing again to how passions can owe more to nurture than nature.)

I met someone recently who loves to bake. She's excellent at it. She loves especially to bake cakes and cupcakes that she can give to neighbors and those in need. Her friends have urged her to turn her baking into a business, and they cannot understand why she would not. Why won't she? Because baking is something she does for sheer love, for relaxation, and for the quiet time it offers her to think, reflect, pray, and commune with God. Not everything we love to do must be turned into money.

Even Paul and Jesus had day jobs.

Consider the legendary story of Steve Jobs dropping out of college, starting a computer business in his garage, and founding Apple, the company that changed the world and all our lives. There's one crucial part of this story that I'd never encountered until reading Cal Newport's *So Good They Can't Ignore You*. Newport explains that Jobs's initial passion had nothing to do with computing, business, or entrepreneurialism. Before stumbling into that part of his life, Jobs spent years on a spiritual quest that took him to India, a Zen training center, and life on a commune. That was the passion he first pursued. What he ended up doing—with passion and excellence—could hardly be, at least on the surface, more opposite. This one example, multiplied many times in other stories, is why Newport believes that the myth of pursuing your passion "not only fails to describe how most people actually end up with compelling careers, but for many people it can actually make things worse: leading to chronic job shifting and unrelenting angst when . . . one's reality inevitably falls short of the dream."[11] Newport's research shows, he argues, that "it's hard to predict in advance what you'll eventually grow to love."[12]

My friend Julie Anne Smith has seen this firsthand. After her marriage ended when she was in her fifties, she needed to find a way to support herself and her children. Her research showed her that cybersecurity was a field in high demand and one in which professionals don't tend to age out. Julie knew nothing about cybersecurity when she began her studies in the field. She actually hated computers and didn't even know how to move the cursor from one monitor to the next. Now, years later, she has grown to love her work as a cybersecurity analyst and finds deep satisfaction in work she knows is relevant and meaningful. And she's good at it.

This idea that you should pursue your passion, what Newport calls the "passion hypothesis," is treated today as a standard formula. But according to Newport, it's not likely to work in the long run. Newport says it is unfortunate that this canard "convinces people that somewhere there's a magic 'right' job waiting for them, and that if they find it, they'll immediately recognize that this is the work *they were meant to do*. The problem, of course, is when they fail to find this certainty, bad things follow, such as chronic job-hopping and crippling self-doubt."[13]

Understanding that there is no magical formula or perfect job just waiting for you can be freeing. Such an understanding encourages you to pursue different interests, develop different skills, and accumulate a range of experiences—and see them all as an ongoing part of pursuing your calling, knowing that God will use it all.

I love the way Samantha Klassen describes this process. Comparing the finding of our vocation to the imperfect and sometimes frustrating process of weaving threads on a loom, Klassen says that in looking back on our life, "we can often see the way our experiences crossed over each other to become part of the whole," like a tapestry or woven cloth. "We see how our vocation is composed of even the threads that, at the time, felt like a complete mistake or a shot in the dark."[14]

I've always advised college students to major in what interests them at this stage in their life, simply because they can. But I also tell them (and their parents) that the majority of college students will change their major. Indeed, the structure of a liberal arts degree is designed to require foundational studies in a variety of subjects that support the second half of the degree, which is focused on a particular discipline. This approach is based on the expectation that being exposed to a range of subjects may lead to the discovery of new interests and abilities—as well as the fact that general knowledge supports particular fields of knowledge. Thus, the core classes required for the degree are not merely ones you "have to take" that you "will never use," as students sometimes complain. Interests may change over time, but most of us are more likely to learn while studying something of interest. So my advice for college students is to major in what you love while you have the chance. My corresponding advice to concerned parents is that it's not necessarily practical to be practical. Most four-year degrees are essentially equal, so the chance to pursue an interest within that context ought not to be squandered. Within the narrow context and short time frame of gaining a four-year degree, pursuing your passion is exactly the right advice (especially in an age in which a college degree has become what a high school diploma was for past generations). At the same time, a lifetime of financial debt is not worth four years of passion, a lesson that has come too late for many young people and those who advised them poorly. There really is no golden ticket to material success. But wise stewardship of all we have been given will always bear good fruit.

As with a taste for coffee, passions are more likely to be developed over time and with experience than to be preexisting. As Newport argues, our identity, our loves, and our passions are complicated, not reducible to black-and-white or yes-or-no answers; so making job, career, and even vocational decisions based on those questions that require yes or no answers alone is not always wise.

Our desires are always being formed and cultivated not only by innate qualities but also by outer sources. Those outer sources include God—who creates all of us as unique beings—and our parents (as in the story by Blackaby), along with our friends, peers, society, social media, art, culture, and ads. So many ads! Are you as easily spurred by a television commercial to crave chicken wings as I am? Do you eventually break down and buy the shoes that keep appearing on websites after you looked them up just one time? So much of what we desire is cultivated by our surrounding culture.

I recall vividly the first time I heard of a young person whose goal was to be a famous YouTuber. I was truly incredulous—Who had ever heard of such a thing?—although now I understand it a (little) bit more. Similarly, I remember being interviewed by a student publication about ten years ago. The student who interviewed me asked how someone could become an "influencer." I thought I was literally being asked how one can have influence on people. I went on and on about building relationships with the people around you, having meaningful conversations, and showing that you listen and care. I was surprised that a young adult didn't know how people have influence on each other. It was some time later when I was introduced to the concept of the "influencer," and I remembered back to that conversation.

Recently, my yoga instructor—who trained in India for a rigorous form of yoga practice that lasts hours each day and is extremely skilled in the practice—observed how she'd be even better at her practice if she'd started when she was five rather than when she was middle-aged. "But no one was doing yoga in rural Virginia in the 1960s," she noted wryly.

The point is that our desires—as well as our passions—are much more externally formed than we might realize. Think about the passions people have today that wouldn't have been possible a century ago or even decades ago, the ones rooted in the newest trends and technology, such as YouTubing and influencing. But history goes back much further than 2010. Did men and women develop a passion to fly airplanes or become an astronaut two hundred years ago? I don't think so. Meanwhile, the number of nuns in America has declined by 76 percent over the last fifty years.[15] The vocation still exists, but something in society has happened to make fewer people want to pursue that particular calling.

Our desires, collectively, are changing.

And that's only natural as the world changes.

The masterpiece of world literature *Don Quixote* is, among other things, the sweet, comic story of a man determined to fulfill his passion for knighthood and chivalry despite the passing of that age. He enlists the assistance of a farmworker to serve as his squire, and the two sally forth on adventures that are rooted more in their wild imaginations than in reality, actions based on the past rather than the present. Like Quixote, we all can find ourselves tilting at windmills from time to time.

Fulfilling our passions and finding our callings depends greatly on the context of our place and time. Some people feel a sense of having been born at the wrong time simply because the way their souls have been formed would better fit another time. But, alas, time travel is not an option. Each of us must find our place in the world where we are.

In my case, my passion to read might be innate. It might be related to how I was wired, how my brain and personality work, how God knit me together in the womb. There is no way to know. But what I do know is that God in his providence had me born in a specific time and place and to parents who could cultivate this passion within me. My mother regularly read to me from the start. My father did, too, sometimes. When I could finally read on my own, I never stopped reading.

But many people in other times and places didn't read because they couldn't. Even if they could, they didn't have easy access to as many books as I have. When I think, for example, about Frederick Douglass determinedly learning to read as an enslaved child at a time in which it was "unlawful as well as unsafe to teach a slave to read,"[16] I cannot imagine my own passion and skill to read coming even close to his. He read as though his life depended on it—because it did. Yet he could have lost his life for doing it. He eventually used these dearly bought skills to become an abolitionist, a reformer, and a preacher, helping to change the course of history.

Circumstances that bring or deny opportunity are at the core of the ten-thousand-hour rule (the idea that becoming excellent at anything requires ten thousand hours of practice), a concept popularized by Malcolm Gladwell's book *Outliers*: one must exist in circumstances that make such practice possible. The simple truth is that many will not even have the opportunity to pursue their passions as intensely as they might wish, while still others will have untapped, unknown potential that their circumstances simply won't bring to the surface.

Thomas Gray's most famous poem, "Elegy Written in a Country Churchyard," published in 1751, addresses this idea. The poem describes an evening scene in the place described in the poem's title: a rustic cemetery outside a rural church. The churchyard holds old gravestones of humble farmers, housewives, laborers, and children, all long laid to rest, those whose lives were spent in hard, anonymous toil (this hamlet's "rude forefathers") until those lives ended, destined to remain forever unknown to the rest of the world.

The poem describes the kind of work that likely filled the days of those buried there:

> For them no more the blazing hearth shall burn,
>   Or busy housewife ply her evening care:
> No children run to lisp their sire's return,
>   Or climb his knees the envied kiss to share.
>
> Oft did the harvest to their sickle yield,
>   Their furrow oft the stubborn glebe has broke;
> How jocund did they drive their team afield!
>   How bow'd the woods beneath their sturdy stroke!

These words give dignity to the labor and lives of these unknown villagers. The poem goes on to chide the ambitious, striving elite of the world who might scorn ordinary rustics like these:

> Let not Ambition mock their useful toil,
>   Their homely joys, and destiny obscure;

> Nor Grandeur hear with a disdainful smile
> > The short and simple annals of the poor.

We arrive at the crux of the whole poem when it suggests that there may be little essential difference between these anonymous souls and the great, remembered names of history beyond their circumstances. Indeed, some who are buried here might also have accomplished what the greatest poets, warriors, and kings in history have done if their circumstances had been different:

> Perhaps in this neglected spot is laid
> > Some heart once pregnant with celestial fire;
> Hands, that the rod of empire might have sway'd,
> > Or wak'd to ecstasy the living lyre.
>
> But Knowledge to their eyes her ample page
> > Rich with the spoils of time did ne'er unroll;
> Chill Penury repress'd their noble rage,
> > And froze the genial current of the soul.
>
> . . . .
>
> Some village-Hampden, that with dauntless breast
> > The little tyrant of his fields withstood;
> Some mute inglorious Milton here may rest,
> > Some Cromwell guiltless of his country's blood.[17]

In other words, there may be among these poor masses of people some who might have had the same innate passions and latent skills of the mighty people known to history, such as the great poet John Milton or the Puritan leader Oliver

Cromwell. But the lives these country folks were born into—called to—left them to live and die in obscurity regardless of what natural, untapped gifts they may have possessed. Just as will happen to most of us who live on this earth.

As Os Guinness explains, "Giftedness does not stand alone in helping us discern our callings. It lines up alongside other factors, such as family heritage, our life opportunities, God's guidance, and our unquestioning readiness to do what he shows."[18]

This hard truth gets to the heart of what it means to be called.

Definitions

Have you ever noticed that the most important words seem to have the most meanings? This fact makes sense when you think about how the most meaningful human concepts have been around for a long time—and have been considered, examined, explored, and contested for just as long. Concepts related to work and our vocational callings have, not surprisingly, accrued many terms that have various meanings and applications. The key to knowing how they are being used is context.

"Vocation" and "calling" are words used in wildly varying contexts. And their meanings can change within those contexts. For example, sometimes in this book I use "vocation" in contrast to "avocation," but my overall argument about vocation is that it transcends profession and pay. A vocation can be fulfilled in a paid or unpaid position. Most of our first vocations, in fact, aren't related to work or career at all. When I was being formed in my mother's womb, God called me to be a daughter to both of my parents and a sister to my two older brothers.

Familial relationships are callings. Later, as a child, the Lord called me to himself, and I became a Christian, the most important calling of all. Marriage, too, is a vocation, as both the Catholic Church and Martin Luther have taught. Some have that calling, and others do not. While the word "calling" has many different applications, the overall sense is the same.

A vocation might begin as a hobby and then become a job or career—or it might be something we devote our whole lives to and never get paid to do or gain public recognition for doing. It can overlap with any of these other categories, but it always transcends them all.

Work—which, as we've seen, is part of what it means to be human and to imitate our Creator through the creative nature of work—can fall into various categories. We do work in many areas of our lives.

In a short video interview, Elizabeth Gilbert, author of *Eat, Pray, Love*, helpfully defines four categories of work: hobby, job, career, and vocation.[1] I'm drawing on Gilbert to describe them briefly here, before fleshing out some of them in the chapters that follow.

Hobby. Gilbert describes hobbies as the interests we pursue purely for pleasure. What makes a hobby fun (even if it requires a lot of effort) is that the "stakes are zero." In pursuing a hobby, you don't have to make money from it, you don't have to attract an audience for it, and you don't have to make a name for yourself. A hobby can be completely for private enjoyment (like my very unskilled flower gardening).

Job. Of the four categories, a job, Gilbert says, is the only one that is a necessity. We all need to have the means to put a roof over our heads and food on the table. Very few of us, she points out, are "landed gentry" these days. Even the vast majority of writers and artists have day jobs. A job doesn't have to be great or fulfilling, she says. It just has to pay. And if a better one comes along, all the better. The things you love in life can be pursued outside a job.

Career. Gilbert defines a career as "a job that you are passionate about and that you love." A career is something worth making sacrifices for because you love it. It's fine to have a job that you hate, Gilbert says, but not a career that you hate. If you don't love your career, you shouldn't have it. I would add to this another helpful distinction between a job and a career: the word "career" comes from a word that means "to run a course." (It shares this root with the word "careen."[2]) By its very definition, a career implies a course, a trajectory, a direction. If your work is taking you along a course that you do not love, it might be time to get off the train before it carries you further and further in the wrong direction.

Vocation. Though she comes from a "spiritual but not religious" perspective, Gilbert essentially agrees with the Christian understanding that vocation is a "divine invitation," a calling from outside ourselves. She describes it as the "voice of the universe in your ear saying, 'I want you to do this thing. I want to use your talents and gifts to make this thing. I want you to participate in the story of creation in this way.'" No one can give your vocation to you (the way a job can be given), and no one can take your vocation from you (the way even a career can be ended by someone or something). Gilbert says that before she had any paying *jobs* as a writer, she had a *vocation* as a writer, working various other jobs in order to pursue her vocation. She acknowledges that the writing career she eventually gained could end someday (whether because people no longer like her work or because the publishing industry itself comes to an end), but she will still write because it is her vocation. It is what "the universe" has called her to do—whether or not anyone sees her do it or pays her to do it.

Gilbert's definition corresponds well with a more scholarly one, which defines calling as "a transcendent summons, experienced as originating beyond the self."[3]

Yes, a "divine invitation."

Calling

When I was eighteen, I carried a vivid picture of what my life would be like when I was twenty-eight. That particular image took form during my first semester of college when my English professor assigned an essay describing what we envisioned our lives would be like ten years from that point in time. I described an evening of horseback riding into the sunset (yes, it's true) with my future husband (whoever he was—I couldn't see his face in this picture—we were facing the sunset, after all) with our two Labrador retrievers ambling alongside. I imagined that my husband and I had been married for five years, that I was established in my career as a social worker (the major I started with in college), and that on that ride we discussed starting a family.

I had it so clearly mapped out.

What's interesting is how much my life turned out as I described it in the essay—and how much it didn't.

I met the man who would become my husband just weeks after writing the essay. We married a year later. (I was nineteen, not twenty-three.) Three semesters later, I changed my major from social work to English. (I would have made a terrible social worker.) I went on to get a PhD in English. We were never able to have children. We did have horses and have owned numerous dogs throughout our decades of marriage. (Never a Labrador retriever though. I have no idea why I thought I would like that breed! No offense to Lab lovers, but they are lumbering and goofy.)

Entering college as a social work major, I took English as a requirement, although it was certainly one I looked forward to. I had loved English throughout all my elementary and high school years. During my second semester in college, my American literature professor encouraged me to switch my major to English. "No," I told him. "English is something I enjoy but not something I take seriously." (Ouch.) Just one semester later, I found myself back in that professor's office. He was the department chair and had to sign the form allowing me to declare my major in English. He hadn't forgotten our earlier conversation, and he was amused to let me know he hadn't. I didn't know it then, but I was on my way to discovering my calling. But it would take a while.

My friend Chris Davis is a pastor. He is one of the most pastoral people I know. People in his home church told him when he was in high school that he was called to ministry. In college he spent his spare time ministering by mentoring younger students, facilitating Bible studies, and preaching in churches. But Chris didn't think he was called to ministry because, in his mind, he had a picture of what a calling looked like: direct from God, accompanied by a feeling inside, followed by a walk up the church aisle to the altar to accept. That didn't happen, so he planned to pursue advanced studies in math after college and become a professor, assuming he would remain involved in church life as he had always done—as a layperson. But then someone who observed how he spent his time asked him if he'd ever considered that he was called to be a pastor since that was what he was already doing. He was taken aback at first. But then he came to understand that this was his call. The call came from God through a wise person in his life. And he answered that call.

Randall Wallace, the screenwriter and film director who is most famous for writing the screenplay for *Braveheart*, had a similar experience but in reverse. Randall grew up in the same Baptist church in central Virginia that my husband and I later attended. As a young man, Randall just sort of assumed that his strong faith and desire to serve the church meant he should be a pastor, so after majoring in religion in college, he headed to divinity school. While in seminary, Randall relates, "I was sitting down with my pastor and he said, 'Do you feel the call to be a pastor?' I said, 'Honestly, I don't, but I know it's the greatest call anyone can have.' And he said, 'You're wrong. The greatest call anyone can ever have is the one God has for you.' It's one of the greatest things anyone ever told me."[1] He left seminary after one year of study and pursued his calling to write great stories. The rest, as they say, is history.

When millennial entrepreneur Kate Kennedy (whom we met in a previous chapter) fell into evangelical church life as a young person, she heard people for the first time speak of being called by God to do certain things. *He calls you?* she wondered. She wanted God to call her, too, in the way she thought people meant. But he didn't.[2] God doesn't just call us on the phone and give us the time, date, and place where we should show up, much as that would make things easier.

So what do we mean when we talk about being called?

Because I'm a word person, I like to start with definitions. The word "vocation" comes from the Latin word from which we also get the word "call," along with the words "vocal" and "vocalization." A call, most literally, is an audible sound, cry, or summons. In this literal sense, a call is a summons of someone by someone else. A call requires both a caller and the called.

A calling from God isn't an audible vocalization such as that given by a military commander or an order from a judge given in court. Rather, God uses the things he has made—other people, our circumstances, our gifts, and even our passions—to sound that call. It is not our job to *be called*. It is our job to *answer* the call. The Bible is replete with stories of people being called. Indeed, within the biblical context and within our own lives, calling is "a metaphor for the life of faith itself."[3] But hearing and discerning this call so that we can answer it isn't always easy. While passion burns inside us, a *call* comes from outside.

Remember that famous line from the classic horror movie *When a Stranger Calls*? "The call is coming from inside the house." If we were our own callers, it would be kind of a horror-movie situation. But understanding that a calling takes place outside ourselves helps us live in the truth that the pressure to be called is not our own.

Passion is inside; a calling comes from outside.

They don't always entirely coincide. But sometimes they do.

Charlotte Brontë's *Jane Eyre* marvelously depicts this distinction. From early in life, Jane's character is defined by a strong sense of justice, a genuine faith, and a fierce desire to love and to be loved. Each of these driving passions meets obstruction after obstruction as Jane seeks to find her way in a lonely and hostile world, to find a place where she belongs. Tempted many times to accept a place or role that is not right for her, Jane finally hears an audible call, a cry from the man she loves from miles and miles away, summoning her back to him in circumstances that now make it right for them to be together. Within the world of the story, it would be impossible for such a call to be carried so far and to be heard by Jane where she is. We can take it only as a supernatural call. But it hardly matters. After many false starts over the course of a difficult and lonely life, Jane's inner passion and her external call finally coincide. *Jane Eyre* is often seen as a kind of modern allegory, a *Pilgrim's Progress* for our own age. In particular, its depiction of the importance of and the distinction between passion and calling offers a striking metaphor for the modern-day search for and fulfillment of calling.

I've seen a different example of passion and calling completely overlapping in the life of my mother. Over many, many decades, my parents have lived in many places and belonged to churches in each one of them. In each of these churches, my mother has had a role in teaching Sunday school, Vacation Bible School, or the children's choir. Even before that, while attending school as a girl in a one-room schoolhouse in rural Maine, she was assigned by her teacher to help instruct the younger students. My mother never went to college to become a teacher, never had a career or a paying job in teaching. Yet she taught for almost her entire life.

The interesting thing, however, is that she realized only a few years ago that she was a teacher, that she had been one all this time, and that being one was her vocation. She had simply done it without that awareness. Even as she approached her nineties and became too frail to attend church in person, she would sit at home making lessons and craft projects to mail out to children in the family and in a ministry halfway across the globe. She simply could not not teach the Bible to children. It was her calling.

You, too, may be able to look back on your life someday (or even now) and see that something you have been doing all along has been all that time a calling—even before you recognized it as one.

In a previous chapter, I observed that being paid to do what you love has, for most of human history, been the exception, not the rule. I admit, gratefully, that for most of my working life, I have been blessed to be one of the exceptions. I acknowledge this. I never imagined in all my growing-up years, with my nose constantly in a book, that I would someday be called to be a professional reader—be called to teach others to read literature, be called to write and speak about literature.

I also mentioned in that chapter that people often ask me how I got where I am, how I do what I do, usually in the context of writing. The answer is that I was called. (Well, strictly speaking, I was usually emailed.) I began my public writing career publishing in small publications, building up my résumé (and, more importantly, honing my craft). Eventually, one editor at a national Christian publication reached out, interested in seeing more of my work and eventually publishing it. As a result of that wider exposure, even bigger national publications, secular ones, reached out, asking me to pitch essays that they eventually published. Nearly all of my greatest writing opportunities came because someone called me. Now, that doesn't mean I didn't try, didn't strive to do excellent work, or didn't place myself in spaces where I might be found. I did. But because I was called, I knew my writing was a calling.

Even if the sense of our calling is felt within, the actual call comes from other people—and ultimately, we trust as believers, from God. God is an external, objective source. He is someone else. We are not him.

So when people tell me they feel called to do something, I want to ask, *Who is calling you?*

Traditionally, within the larger context of church history, "calling" or "vocation" referred to one's role in full-time church ministry, whether as a nun, monk, priest, or pastor. These terms are still sometimes used that way when, for example, people refer to a full-time church job as "vocational ministry" (as opposed to the "lay ministry" of someone in the laity) or a minister who has a second job outside the church is called a "bivocational pastor."

However, the Protestant Reformation challenged the traditional distinction between secular and sacred vocations. The Reformers understood that God calls everyone—not just to full-time ministry but to all kinds of work—and that other work can be a vocation too.

Martin Luther's views on vocation, in particular, were tremendously influential. They were directly connected to his understanding of salvation by faith alone and have been summed up as saying, "God doesn't need your good works, but your neighbor does."[4] For Luther, any kind of work is vocational when you are called by God to do it. Such roles aren't limited to nine-to-five jobs; callings include those of mother, father, daughter, son, citizen, and church member, as well as truck driver, farmer, teacher, and shop owner.

Nevertheless, even within some decidedly Protestant contexts (I'm thinking of my own evangelical world, in particular), the elevated status of "full-time ministry" lingers. One speaker at the 2024 Pastors' Conference of the Southern Baptist Convention declared the role of pastor to be "the highest calling on the planet."[5] This persistent assumption that church work is higher or nobler than "worldly" work (a form of neomonasticism)[6] is the source of all kinds of evil. With all due respect to my monastic friends, a view of calling that puts "spiritual" work above other kinds of roles distorts our understanding of both ministry and work.

David Rowe has it right. As a school chaplain, he had been talking to a student at his school's graduation who said she felt God was calling her to be an accountant. He later posted on social media: "I was so excited. I've never in my life heard someone say that before."

We should hear more of this!

A friend of mine, for example, found herself trying to discern a new direction for her vocation after leaving a church job she loved following the church's mishandling of abuse. She had prepared her whole life to work in and for the church, including going to seminary. The disillusionment she experienced over the situation in the church made her want to seek work outside the church. She struggled not to feel like she would be giving up her calling and even wasting her hard-earned seminary degree. Yet seeking to use her gifts outside the church walls was not necessarily a change in vocation. Nor would her theological education be wasted. Every Christian is called to "full-time ministry," regardless of who signs the paycheck (or even whether there is a paycheck). She ended up taking a teaching position at a school—and teaching was exactly what she had been doing in the church. Her vocation didn't change; her setting did. Situations and jobs can change even as our vocation remains the same.

Vocations are like roles: we can serve the same role in a variety of life and work circumstances, but at times the roles can shift. When I decided to walk away from my decades-long career as an English professor, I had to wrestle with the question of whether that meant my vocation had ended. In one sense, it did. But in another, I have continued to teach, though in different ways.

While a calling might take a different form, sometimes callings do actually end. And new callings emerge.

The vocation of being a husband or a wife may end with the death of a spouse, for example. A life-altering injury may end the calling of a superathlete. The financial adviser who retires after forty-five years of helping people manage their money may never want to look at a spreadsheet again and may become a writer instead. A friend of mine who became a quadriplegic following a tragic accident developed the astounding talent of painting by holding the brush in her mouth. She has a new calling as an artist, one that did not exist before she experienced her life-changing injuries.

Your calling isn't just about you.

The doctrine of vocation is a robust acknowledgment of the truth that God intended human beings to provide for each other through each other's work. Rather than providing manna from heaven, as he once did, God uses the work of farmers, bakers, truck drivers, and grocers to feed us. Rather than creating each new person from the dust of the earth, God has chosen to use the vocations of husbands and wives, fathers and mothers, to create new human beings. Thus, as Gene Edward Veith explains in *God at Work*, the doctrine of vocation is both "a theology of ordinary life" and "a comprehensive doctrine of the Christian life, having to do with faith and sanctification, grace and good works." Indeed, the ultimate test of whether we are being called to something, Veith says, is to ask, "How does my calling serve my neighbor?"[7]

When someone calls, it means they have a need they think you can fill. This is the heart of vocation. Vocation is not about being able to fulfill our desires, pursue our passions, or follow our bliss. Vocation is about being called by others to serve. This understanding offers a much bigger vision of vocation than mere self-fulfillment. Indeed, Os Guinness argues that "by drastically reducing the immensity of its significance to our individual lives alone," we also diminish our understanding of calling itself and of what it means to be called by God.[8]

Fulfillment is like happiness in this way. Happiness, says Viktor Frankl—writing following his miraculous survival after being imprisoned in four Nazi concentration camps—"cannot be pursued; it must ensue, and it only does so as the unintended side-effect of one's dedication to a cause greater than oneself or as the product of one's surrender to a person other than oneself. Happiness must happen."[9]

What Andrew Peterson says about art in *Adorning the Dark* might just be true of all callings: "Art shouldn't be about self-expression or self-indulgence. Art shouldn't be about self. . . . The aim ought to be for the thing to draw attention ultimately to something other than the Self."[10] As Christians, we know what that ultimate other thing should be. The irony, Peterson points out, is that "we are most ourselves when we are thinking least about ourselves."[11]

65

There's a neat illustration of this perspective in the book *Make Your Job a Calling*. The story is told of a driver who came upon a traffic jam amid some road construction on a long, two-lane highway in the mountains. The road was teeming with late-afternoon traffic because one lane was closed. Just as this driver was about to be let through, the flagman turned his sign around to the stop side, and the driver found himself at the head of the new line next to the flagman and settled in for a long wait. The driver began to talk to the flagman—someone whose job it was to stand there all day, day in and day out, in all kinds of weather—and asked him how he could tolerate such a boring job. Imagine the driver's surprise when the flagman replied, "I love this job! Love it. You know why? Because it matters. I keep people safe. I care about these guys behind me, and I keep them safe. I also keep you safe, and everybody else in all those cars behind you. I get to make a real, tangible difference every day."[12]

Oddly enough, in a time when we've diminished the concept of vocation, we also tend to define ourselves by our work. "What do you do?" is one of the first questions we ask upon meeting a new person (a particularly American tic).[13] We are a work-centric culture even when, perhaps especially when, we lack a sense of vocation.

Vocation includes work, but it is more than just a career, job, or source of income.

Jennifer Wiseman is an astronomer who studies the continuing formation of stars. I met Jennifer at a conference, and we ended up talking about our mutual love of animals. She grew up on a farm with livestock and wildlife and, like me, has had various companion animals throughout her life. While her work right now centers on her role on the Hubble Space Telescope oversight team, she startled me when she said making animals happy is one of her callings. She's never worked professionally with animals and doesn't have any pets right now, but even so, she says, "Whether it's helping a worm on the asphalt get back to its natural soil, or doing what I can to help wildlife and animals in farms and labs be treated with holistic mercy and respect, it is perhaps the strongest yearning deep within my soul." For Jennifer, this is a calling. It is far more than a source of income and more than just something she does on a regular basis; it's part of who she is.

Vocation is one way you fulfill your purpose, the role (or roles) for which you were created.

A job or career can be something that helps you fulfill the larger calling on your life. Part of this reality is that not everything we choose to do (or not do) fits into our true calling.

I was called to the academic life; of that I am sure. From the time I was a little girl to the end of my twenty-five years as a professor, I adored being in school, and I flourished there as both a student and a professor. More importantly, I believe I served others well there. When I was a student, like most students, I took on a variety of jobs—restaurant server, horse farm worker, and tutor—but none of these were my *callings*. They were means by which I could pursue my calling during those years.

Note, too, that those jobs I held as a means to fulfill my own calling could be callings for other people. I think, for example, of the breeders, owners, and trainers I worked under at the horse farm, people who devoted their lives to those animals (and taught me so much through their callings). I think of the restaurant owners and cooks who devoted their lives to the food industry. I was just one more college waitress passing through, but some of them were called to that work.

It's helpful to think about all the roles we can fill that aren't necessarily callings. Jesus had a calling, and he worked as a builder as part of following that call. Paul had a calling, too, and he worked as a tentmaker to provide for himself and his ministry. There are people out there whose primary calling *is* builder or tentmaker. Any kind of work can be a calling for one person but just a job for another. The difference isn't the work itself. The difference is in who you are and who God is calling you to be. Some roles might support our callings as temporary assignments, or perhaps they are roles we mistake for a calling. That's a more difficult dilemma to consider, but we must do so.

We all know people serving in roles for which they are so ill-fitted that they seem to be role-playing, badly, at something they wish they could do. I don't mean to make light of this, because with some positions—teaching and pastoring come most immediately to mind—others can be harmed in the process of doing work one is not called by God (or intrinsic nature) to do. In the realm of creative work, which is inherently more subjective, we've all encountered people desperately trying to be called to sing, play, perform, or write. When the calls don't come, it might be owing to any number of things: too little need (market) for a particular talent, not yet finding the right audience for a form of art, or insufficient talent. That last one is hardest to come to grips with, because most of us aren't going to come out and say that to someone. The burden is really on ourselves to seek and receive honest feedback on whatever we are doing, whether to improve or to realize it may not be our calling. I took years of piano lessons as a girl before I realized I was no good at playing piano, and I stopped. I really wasn't good! But no one told me. Certainly not the teachers getting paid to give me lessons. I had to figure it out on my own. Sometimes we just aren't called to the things we wish we were called to.

On the other hand, people will leave a role and explain their departure by saying God has "called" them elsewhere. At times, I wish they'd simply say, "Hey, I decided I want to do this new thing." Because surely that is the case at times.

Sometimes the call really is coming from inside the house. But it can be hard to see that, let alone say it.

Life is long and full. We do lots of things and take on many different tasks and roles. It might be that only in looking backward or amid a crisis or turning point do we see the way in which all the aspects are woven together into a kind of tapestry that depicts our true callings.

It's also good to enjoy doing things that you aren't good at and that aren't centrally connected to your calling. (Remember my love for running—and that I'm very, very slow and, therefore, definitely not good at it?) Complications arise when one assumes that passion or enjoyment equals calling, as we've already seen.

One plotline in *The Office* fleshes out these distinctions between calling, passion, and hobbies. (Of course, the central idea of *The Office* is that everyone working at Dunder Mifflin, a paper supply company, is doing anything but pursuing a passion—and yet they somehow find fulfillment and purpose there.) A central scene within this subplot takes place when Pam, who is engaged to Jim and enrolled in art school, decides with Jim's brothers to pull a prank on him. Pam wants to pretend she lost her engagement ring, but Jim's brothers commandeer the idea and decide the prank should be to mock Pam's pursuit of a career in art in front of Jim by teasing that "she basically has a hobby for a job."[14] As is usual for *The Office*, the whole thing is awkward and painful as the mockery reveals Pam's insecurities. Yet the way the overarching plotline develops throughout the series subtly shows that Pam hopes to be an artist—yet lacks both the drive and the talent that it would take. She is not called to be an artist. Yet art remains a hobby for her as she finds her real calling and gladness working in the office with the people she loves and eventually creating a family with Jim. It's a beautiful—and poignant—picture of a person learning about the realities of work, her own limitations, and—most importantly—what she really loves and takes joy in.

Perhaps by understanding the important distinction between passion and calling, we can have clearer categories for both and for their relationship to each other. And who knows? Persistence might pay off. Sometimes the right connection at the right moment between caller and called can take an excruciating amount of time—or planning (the way some parents and coaches make sure their kids and players will be seen by scouts).

Remember Sarah from a previous chapter? Well, it turns out she is a very gifted writer. And she did get her book published, despite people like me not offering strong encouragement.[15] Looking back and reflecting on her persistence and patience despite the obstacles, Sarah told me:

> It helped that . . . I had received other messages from writers who knew my work, telling me that I *was* a good writer, and I ought to persevere. But I do think it was also helpful to receive your words as a reminder that my calling wasn't going to be evident to everyone . . . and neither could it be nullified by anyone else. It was mine.[16]

And then there are those who are called to something but do not feel passionate about that calling—and might even resist it.

One of my favorite examples of someone called and not at all happy about it comes from "The Collar," another poem by George Herbert. The speaker of the poem, as we gradually understand in reading along, is a minister, a man who wears a collar. At first we don't know whom he is speaking to, but his speech turns out to be a long monologue delivered in a fit of temper to God. The poem begins with him striking a table and saying, "No more!" He "will abroad," meaning he's hitting the road, getting out, giving up:

> I struck the board, and cried, "No more;
> >   I will abroad!
> What? shall I ever sigh and pine?
> My lines and life are free, free as the road,
> Loose as the wind, as large as store.
> >   Shall I be still in suit?
> Have I no harvest but a thorn
> To let me blood, and not restore
> What I have lost with cordial fruit?
> >   Sure there was wine
> Before my sighs did dry it; there was corn
> >   Before my tears did drown it.
> >   Is the year only lost to me?
> >   Have I no bays to crown it,
> No flowers, no garlands gay? All blasted?
> >   All wasted?
> Not so, my heart; but there is fruit,
> >   And thou hast hands.
> Recover all thy sigh-blown age
> On double pleasures: leave thy cold dispute
> Of what is fit and not. Forsake thy cage,
> >   Thy rope of sands,
> Which petty thoughts have made, and made to thee
> Good cable, to enforce and draw,
> >   And be thy law,
> While thou didst wink and wouldst not see.

> Away! take heed;
> I will abroad.
> Call in thy death's-head there; tie up thy fears;
> He that forbears
> To suit and serve his need
> Deserves his load."
> But as I raved and grew more fierce and wild
> At every word,
> Methought I heard one calling, *Child!*
> And I replied *My Lord*.[17]

Frustrated and disappointed at the lack of harvest for his labors, angry at God for seemingly not seeing his toil and despair, anxious and angry about the failures in his work and ministry, the speaker sputters and rages, line after line, accusation after accusation. He stops only when he hears the God he is addressing reply with one simple word: "Child." And the called responds to the Caller (notice the pun on "collar"), "My Lord."

What a picture of true calling. God's call "is not the echo of my nature," Oswald Chambers says, in an echo of Herbert's poem. Rather, God's nature can overcome our own limited nature:

> When we speak of the call of God, we are apt to forget the most important feature, viz., the nature of the One Who calls. There is the call of the sea, the call of the mountains, the call of the great ice barriers; but these calls are only heard by the few. The call is the expression of the nature from which it comes, and we can only record the call if the same nature is in us. The call of God is the expression of God's nature, not of our nature.

The "threading of God's voice to us," as Chambers describes it, weaves together the unique particularities of our individuality and our circumstances, allowing us to hear that call. Chambers explains, "There are strands of the call of God providentially at work for us which we recognize and no one else does." Indeed, Chambers says (as is captured in Herbert's poem), "To be brought into the zone of the call of God is to be profoundly altered."[18]

The idea of George Herbert, a seventeenth-century Cambridge-educated priest, experiencing such a clear sense of calling is one thing. But how are we ordinary folks in this frenzied modern world, which brings us so many choices, supposed to hear our calling amid all the noise? (By the way, not even Herbert followed a straight path to his ultimate vocation: he served in Parliament earlier in life and didn't enter the priesthood until his thirties. Herbert is now mainly remembered for his poetry, most of which wasn't published until after his death.) As Dorothea Brooke says in *Middlemarch* (a novel that deals with calling in very interesting ways), "After all, people may really have in them some vocation which is not quite plain to themselves, may they not?" When it comes to finding our calling, Dorothea continues, "We should be very patient with each other, I think."[19] And, I would add, we should be patient with ourselves.

God often uses others to deliver his calling on our life. Recognizing this fact leads to two important insights.

First, one way we can discern our calling is to listen to wise people around us who know us and who can see qualities, gifts, and potentials we often don't see in ourselves. Our talents, whether natural or cultivated (usually both), play a big part in both discerning and fulfilling our calling. There's a trite saying among Christians that "God doesn't call the equipped; he equips the called." Now, surely God does equip those he calls. Exodus 31 describes how God equipped Bezalel and Oholiab with the artisanal skills to design, build, and adorn the tabernacle. But the idea that the less competent you are for a role, the more God is glorified is not wisdom. Proverbs 18:16 says that your gifts will make room or open doors for you. The pattern set forth in Scripture is that God gives the gifts, and then the doors open. That is how we know we are called.

Because we live in a fallen world, there will be times when others' sin is the reason you are not called to use your gifts. It may very well be that your gifts are being ignored or underused because of someone else's greed, jealousy, fear, prejudice, or any number of wrong motives or ill conceptions. This subject could warrant an entire book, but for my purposes here, I want to say that even if this is true (and sometimes we suspect it but don't really know for certain), you ought to listen for a call from elsewhere. Many of us desire to use our gifts in one particular context—our workplace, our church, or our friend group, for example. If our gift is not wanted there despite our most generous offering of it, then we should seek a place that does want it. This doesn't necessarily mean leaving your workplace or your church or your friend group, but it does mean looking for other rooms. In our Father's mansion, there are many rooms, after all. Don't get stuck in one room. This is a lesson I've had to learn for myself, so I state it earnestly and from experience. On the other hand, we ought not stay in an unhealthy place simply because we are allowed to use our gifts or given a platform there. I know someone who acknowledges how unhealthy her church is yet chooses to stay because she and her husband get to use their gifts there. As human beings, we certainly have an innate need for significance, but that's exactly why we must guard against making decisions based on our need to feel important.

Sometimes our callings do end when the caller ceases to call. I'm writing this following the abrupt and unwanted end to my calling in academia in a turn of events resulting from other people's shortcomings, even their sin. It has been a painful and hard experience. Yet my larger purpose of teaching and learning continues, even if this particular call has ended. Only time and discernment will tell.

Second, there is a reverse side to this role that others play in us finding our own callings: we need, actively and proactively, to help others hear their call. We do that by naming the gifts and strengths we see in them that they might not see themselves. We can encourage and support others to lean into their talents. The world needs people who have a particular giftedness to use those gifts. So many of us are still trying to figure things out, make decisions, and choose a direction. You might never know how a simple offer of encouragement or affirmation of someone else's true gifts and abilities will help them find or stay true to their calling.

I know how helpful it has been for me. Early in my adulthood, my pastor encouraged me to speak publicly at a time when I struggled even to stand up in church during a Sunday evening service to give a testimony (as was customary in the churches of my youth). Teaching and writing are my passions, and they come more easily to me. But speaking has continued to be something I'm called to do. I'm not passionate about speaking. I don't even think I'm that good at it—not in the riveting, polished way of TED Talk speakers. You know the kind I'm talking about. I also find traveling and being away from home just plain hard. Yet, as long as people call, I will answer the call—partly because it helps support my writing (which makes it part of the job) but also because I'm being called by others, at least for now, to serve in this way.

Now, we can still find joy in vocations that are not perfectly aligned with our passions or desires. When God plants desires in us, those desires can serve as a compass to give us direction. You may remember Frederick Buechner's famous definition of vocation: "The place God calls you to is the place where your deep gladness and the world's deep need meet."[20] But deep gladness isn't necessarily the same thing as passion. As Christians—or even just decent people—it is possible and desirable and even simply human to delight in helping others, to be glad to be of help. "The moral will of God determines that each believer should use his gift for the common good."[21]

Thus, the doctrine of vocation emphasizes what God does through our work rather than what we do.[22] We give our best efforts, and the failures, as well as the successes, are ultimately God's business. Such failures are exactly what the speaker in "The Collar" is struggling with. The doctrine of vocation turns the usual question on its head. "Instead of 'what job shall I choose?' the question becomes 'what is God calling me to do?'"[23]

In *Courage and Calling*, Gordon Smith draws on the different gifts and callings described by Paul in Romans 12:6–8 to show how even the specific way in which we view the world as broken reflects the giftings God has given us. The prophet thinks the world needs truth; the teacher sees the world as needing to learn; the servant notices unmet needs. Discerning your vocation comes, in part, from seeing the specific ways in which you *feel* the brokenness of the world.[24] Meeting that need in the world through your specific gifts can bring you deep gladness—even if it's not always fun.

Sometimes saying yes to a call means saying no to something else.

Kate Kennedy, the millennial entrepreneur who never got that phone call from God, thinks that giving up or saying no can be just as much a part of finding your calling as saying yes. She didn't follow along with the common admonition to "never give up." Instead, she writes, "I was defined just as much by the things I quit as the things I did."[25] Figuring out that something isn't working and giving it up is like realizing that the caller on the other end of the line got the wrong number. Or made a butt-dial. It happens.

But if calling consists, in part, of being called by someone (not just ourselves) to serve a role the caller thinks we are equipped to fill, saying no gets trickier. This is especially true in a Christian context where certain built-in assumptions about service and sacrifice, along with guilt about not serving or sacrificing, can become part of the equation.

Early in our marriage, my husband and I attended a wonderful little country church whose people and ministries we adored. It wasn't long, however, before we—the new, young couple—were being asked to teach Sunday school, chaperone the teen overnighters, and drive the church bus. We did all that—and more. Decades later, we still haven't recovered from the burnout. We didn't know enough then to say no.

By no means do I think our little church meant harm or intended to be poor stewards. But in the many years that have passed, I've seen the devastation wrought by people and institutions that, through manipulation and guilt, exploit earnest people within a system built by cheap labor and cultish loyalty. Such systems aren't always built that way on purpose (human nature and human institutions are more complex than that). But calling is such a precious and powerful gift of God that—like all such gifts—it can easily be twisted and distorted if we do not guard it carefully, both our own callings and those of others. Indeed, "no truth is more manipulable than calling when it is corrupted."[26]

Every day we face choices, invitations, tasks, and opportunities. In the context of vocation, these are called daily callings. Such responsibilities won't necessarily develop into a larger, overarching calling, but they must be met.

On the other hand, some things that you might not see as your calling can develop into one, particularly if you continue down the path it sets you on. A college student who works at a fast-food chain while in school may discover a career that turns into a calling within the restaurant business. The farm kid pining to get away from the daily chores he's assigned by his parents may head off to college only to return to the family homestead with a degree in hand, called to bring his new knowledge to the old ways.

Being aware that daily tasks can turn into callings helps us steward those responsibilities differently. It might mean saying yes to an opportunity without the expectation that it will develop into anything more. It might mean saying no because of the possibility that it could become more, because that's not a direction we want to go.

For example, when I was a young professor, popular with students and recognized by my university with its highest teaching award, my dean asked me to help develop courses for the school's burgeoning online enterprise. I was fresh and uncertain enough to assume I wasn't in a place to say no, so I agreed. Then my department chair heard about it. He knew me, knew my gifts, and knew I would hate everything required of creating online courses: technologically, pedagogically, and personally. My gifts were in classroom teaching. He marched into our dean's office and told the boss I wasn't doing it. So someone else was recruited. In the end, it really didn't matter to the school who did the online development. But it mattered tremendously to my life and my calling not to go down that road. I am so grateful I had an advocate to speak up for me when I didn't know to do so for myself.

Sometimes people call you to fill a need because you would be able to fill that need well. And that might be true. But that doesn't mean you're the only one or even the best one to do it. Sometimes the honor in being asked makes it hard to say no. But it can also be wiser, for whatever reasons, to do exactly that—say no.

You also shouldn't allow yourself to bear guilt for or be manipulated into taking on a role that interferes with your true calling or your greater responsibilities. Remember that "the need does not determine the call," as Gordon Smith points out. Of course, we should strive to be as generous as we can and to have compassion. But, as Smith says, "people of vocational integrity do not let the myriad needs around them derail them from fulfilling their vocation."[27]

Let's summarize what we've considered to this point. We've seen that work is good, though often hard. Passion is not the same thing as calling. You don't always get paid to do what you love. Jobs and careers are not the same thing as callings. Vocation is greater than your work. Yet it takes work (whether paid or unpaid) to fulfill your vocation. And you don't have to be passionate about the work itself to be passionate about the calling. Like all good gifts from God, callings can be abused or exploited by others, even ourselves. Our callings must be stewarded well. Callings can take different forms. Some callings can end. And most crucially, a calling requires a caller.

With all these questions, caveats, and concerns, how on earth are you supposed to find your calling?

I'm afraid I have no secret formula, surefire plan, or *six steps to success in finding your one true calling!* I'm sorry.

But I can point you in the right direction. I can point you to truth, goodness, and beauty.

I believe that if you pursue truth, goodness, and beauty in all your work, all your play, all your ways, and all your days, you will find your calling. In fact, I think pursuing truth, goodness, and beauty *is* your calling. It's my calling. It's everyone's calling.

The Transcendentals

Some things are so good and so right that they need no defense or justification. Philosophers refer to these inarguable, universal goods as ultimate values. In fact, goodness itself is one such ultimate value. Goodness, as well as truth and beauty, are the properties of being that philosophers call transcendentals. "Properties of being" is the philosophical way of saying that all things that exist have characteristics that define their very existence or being.

Truth, goodness, and beauty are qualities of God's being, of his nature. He is their ultimate source. The fact that they are three is not coincidental. The world is full of reflections of God's trinitarian nature. And just as the trinitarian God is three persons in one, these three transcendentals exist in unity (which is another, lesser-known transcendental). The transcendental of unity means that truth, goodness, and beauty cannot exist apart from each other. Something cannot be beautiful without also being good and true. It cannot be good if not also beautiful and true. And so on. They are three in one.

The transcendentals are the ideal qualities for all things that exist. There is no being that one would not rightly desire to be a good, true, and beautiful form of that thing. A chair, for example, has properties of existence (or being) that make it a chair. A good chair does the work of being a chair well. It is true to its purpose and looks good doing it. (A chair that looks like a potato peeler would not likely do its job all that well.) All its qualities are unified so as to make it an excellent chair. Obviously, there is a wide range of ways a chair might be and still be a good chair. The same is true of a good dog. A good dog fulfills its purpose of simply being a dog (especially *your* dog) well. There are billions of stars in Earth's galaxy. Only one of these is the star we call the sun. The sun is good in the way it makes life as we know it possible. It is true because it remains each day where we can see it rise and set from wherever we are, day in and day out, without fail. And while doing this so truly and well, it is beautiful. Not only that, but it generates even more beauty by its mere existence. For chairs, dogs, suns, and all things in existence, a vast range of qualities are possible for each thing to be good, true, and beautiful in its own way—while still being what it is.

These transcendentals apply to people too. They *especially* apply to people. To pursue all three is to embrace the reality of what it means to be human—and the virtue or excellence of being human. To reject any of these is to diminish our humanity, the essence of which is the very image of God. We long for truth, goodness, and beauty because, being made in God's image, we long for him.

As absolute, eternal ideals, these transcendentals exist apart from our finite humanity. At the same time, they are the end of all human longing. Even the ancient, pre-Christian philosophers (who first identified these concepts) knew this. The writers of the Bible knew it too. Indeed, Paul echoes the language of the Greek philosophers (whose work he knew) when, in Philippians 4:8, he writes, "Finally, brothers and sisters, whatever is true, whatever is noble, whatever is right, whatever is pure, whatever is lovely, whatever is admirable—if anything is excellent or praiseworthy—think about such things."[1]

Each of the transcendentals reflects a particular aspect of our shared humanity. Human beings are, among all creatures on earth, unique in possessing reason (the ability to discern truth), moral agency (the ability to discern goodness), and aesthetic capacity (the ability to discern beauty). Put differently, truth is the aim of our intellect. Goodness expresses our moral will. Beauty speaks to our aesthetic sense. We pursue truth in our thinking. We pursue goodness in our doing. We pursue beauty through our senses and in our feeling. To cultivate these abilities is to pursue what the ancient philosophers described as the good life—or what Jesus called the abundant life (John 10:10).

The transcendentals lead us to God and to one another. They allow one image bearer of God to commune with another. As Jacques Maritain says,

> The moment one touches a transcendental, one touches being itself, a likeness of God, an absolute, that which ennobles and delights our life; one enters into the domain of the spirit. It is

> remarkable that men really communicate with one another only by passing through being or one of its properties. Only in this way do they escape from the individuality in which matter encloses them. If they remain in the world of their sense needs and of their sentimental egos, in vain do they tell their stories to one another, they do not understand each other. They observe each other without seeing each other, each one of them infinitely alone, even though work or sense pleasures bind them together. But let one touch the good and Love, like the saints, the true, like an Aristotle, the beautiful, like a Dante or a Bach or a Giotto, then contact is made, souls communicate.[2]

Even as the transcendentals are part of our shared human nature, there are also particular ways in which the true, good, and beautiful manifest in our own individual lives. They connect to qualities or properties of being that are unique to each person. They make *you* good at being *you*, and *me* good at being *me*.

In *Break, Blow, Burn, and Make: A Writer's Thoughts on Creation*, E. Lily Yu offers a brilliant illustration of how important it is for us to accept and pursue our unique callings:

> The present state of Christianity might be said to resemble a rehearsal room full of toppled chairs and music stands, where a determined clarinetist and two violas are trying to follow the conductor's baton. In the back of the room, ignoring the conductor, a marimba player bangs out the latest pop hit. Meanwhile, a hundred violinists are brawling in the hall.

Yu continues, "Orchestras do need many violins." But not everyone needs to be a violinist. Indeed, when everyone becomes a violinist, there is no orchestra. "Imagine the kind of faith," Yu writes, that the percussionist needs in order "to wait thirty or fifty or a hundred measures of rest, and at the right moment, eyes never leaving the baton, to strike the two notes on a triangle that complete the praise song of the universes."[3]

In the orchestra of the world, some of us are clarinets, some are violins, some are triangles. We all play our parts. And some of us have to wait a hundred measures of rest before we do so.

Calling, obviously, is part of our becoming who we are supposed to be.

To find and live within your calling is to find and live in truth, goodness, and beauty.

At the same time, the reverse is so: we are all called to pursue truth, goodness, and beauty. We are called to pursue these in all we do and all we are. In fact, I don't think it's possible to pursue your calling without pursuing truth, goodness, and beauty.

The following chapters will explain why.

The True

What does it mean to pursue truth in our callings?

It means at least four things: thinking about truth itself, knowing the truth about ourselves, knowing the truth about the work we might be called to do, and walking in truth in all that we do.

Let's begin by thinking about what truth is. Bear with me here. I'm going to wax a wee bit philosophical for a while, but then we'll get down to brass tacks.

Christians today talk (and write and blog and tweet and opine and pontificate) a lot about truth. We do so not so much because the Bible speaks a lot about truth (it does) but because relativism (which rejects absolute truth) has become so deeply embedded within modern culture. In response, we often feel the need to take up the defense of truth. That's a good thing.

The True

But this reactionary approach leaves goodness and beauty neglected. For example, it's become commonplace to repeat the axiom "All truth is God's truth." (It's actually one of my own favorite sayings!) Yet how often, if ever, do you hear, "All goodness is God's goodness"? Or "All beauty is God's beauty"? These assertions are equally true, since God is the ultimate source of truth, goodness, and beauty. But these parallel ideas are seldom, if ever, expressed. Given our finitude, it is merely human for us to find that when we turn our attention to one thing, we neglect something else. But I would argue that a proper defense of any one of these three ultimate values requires equal attention to all. And the fact is that the notion of beauty being subjective (completely in the eye of the beholder) preceded (and contributed to) the idea that truth is subjective.[1] Since there is no truth apart from goodness and beauty, any attempt to defend truth without the others is doomed to fail. Perhaps this helps explain why even Christians are increasingly succumbing to the relativism of our post-truth culture. Apart from goodness and beauty, we, too, will inevitably fall prey to the very relativism we aim to counter.

So what is truth?

Pontius Pilate asked this question before condemning Jesus to the cross. I think he really wanted to know! Pilate posed the question in response to Jesus telling him that the reason he was born and came into the world was to "testify to the truth" (John 18:37–38). To be human is to long for truth—even if we are easily deceived, even deceived by ourselves. "We want to know, just as we want health, friendship, and love."[2]

We must seek truth in order to live lives that correspond to the world as it is.³

Truth is a lot of things. It is freedom. It is the way in which we are to walk. It is a belt that girds us. It is both spirit and flesh. Truth is life that defeats death, and it is light that overcomes darkness. Jesus is the truth.⁴ This means that truth is a person. And if we are supposed to be like Jesus, then that means that the more we are like him, the more we are like truth itself.

The phrase "Be true to yourself" gets a bad rap. Certainly, it can be used in a way that is based not in truth but in pure subjectivity, with no anchor or mooring beyond the feeling or impulse of the moment.

But for the Christian who believes that God knit each of us together in the womb, with a purpose, a calling, and, yes, a personality, being true to yourself, as God made you to be, is how truth can be a person—how a person can be himself or herself truthfully.

Truth is more than an abstraction. Truth is truest when it is embodied and made real in flesh and blood. You likely know people who are so authentic, who live with so much integrity in terms of who they are, how they live, and how they treat other people, that you just know they are *true*.

Truth doesn't change, but our understanding of what truth is and how we know it does change from age to age and in each of us over time and as we gain experience.

For example, Christians living in today's late-modern age have anxieties about truth that weren't necessarily shared by people in other times and places. The Enlightenment changed the way we view truth. Consider the dramatic shift in the meaning of the word "science" that took place after the Enlightenment. From ancient through medieval times, the word meant "knowledge" or "learning" in any area of study or skill—it encompassed all knowledge. But after the Scientific Revolution (which, according to the old use of the word, means a revolution in *knowledge*), the word came to mean a very specific *kind* of knowledge—namely, empirical, testable, verifiable facts related to the material world,[5] what the ancients had once called natural philosophy. We can see the revolution in an entire worldview through the simple shift in a word's meaning. Essentially, what now counts as knowledge is only the scientific kind.

Yet there is so much more to knowledge and truth than scientific facts. The implications for how we understand truth, therefore, are vast.

When Jesus told parables, no one questioned whether there really was a farmer who sowed seeds, some of which fell on rock and some that did not. Everyone knew that the truth Jesus was communicating was beyond the literal level of the story. Many centuries later, John Bunyan was so anxious about being accused of writing fiction in *The Pilgrim's Progress* that he wrote a long preface in verse to explain that he was writing allegory, not fiction. The distinction between fiction and nonfiction (made-up stories and factual ones) is a modern one. These categories reflect the modern view that the difference between facts and nonfacts is central to knowing the truth.

Yet the ancient philosophers, Plato chief among them, knew that truth "is to be found not only in empirical study of the physical world, but in contemplation of the transcendent goodness which stands behind the material universe."[6] This means that truth exists beyond our own individual, subjective experience of the world, whether in its material forms or in our emotional, spiritual, or intellectual experience of it. Truth helps us know what to make of those facts, how to put them together and apply them. Truth helps us make meaning, something we do simply because we are human. Birds are the nest-making animal. Fish are the water-breathing animal. Cats are the claw-kneading animal. Human beings are the meaning-making animal.

Indeed, our "search for meaning is the primary motivation" in life, writes Viktor Frankl.[7]

We were made to seek truth. We were made to find meaning. For the philosophers of the pre-Christian world, the material world points to the transcendent truths beyond the material. For the Christian, this means that all of creation points to the truth.

If all of creation points to the truth, that means all of creation is pointing to the truth of your calling. The meaning of your vocation does not depend solely on the work itself. Meaning is found by the one who searches it out. One person can read a poem and get nothing out of it. But a careful, inquisitive, and able reader finds riches upon riches in the same poem.

In the beginning was a Poem.

The truths of material reality and transcendent reality are joined in the incarnation. The God who became flesh and dwelled among us is the *logos*, a Greek word whose multiple meanings include "truth." Viktor Frankl offers the definition as simply "meaning."[8]

This word, used in the Gospel of John to name Christ, already existed in the ancient Greek world. It was a word used by philosophers to refer to a concept of "universal divine reason." This reason could be seen in nature, but it also transcended the material world. It referred to an "eternal and unchanging truth present from the time of creation, available to every individual who seeks it."[9] In Jesus the invisible becomes visible. The transcendental ideal of "good" becomes real, present, tangible, and very good. Jesus is truth. But, in his incarnation, death, burial, and resurrection, he also becomes fact.

Yet, because truth is also transcendent—eternal, absolute, and universal—we will never grasp it completely in our finite, subjective, and individual selves.

Another (better) way of saying this is simply, "The fear of the LORD is the beginning of knowledge" (Prov. 1:7). We don't know what God knows. And we need to respect that, even fear it. I don't know anything about flying airplanes. I would definitely fear taking the controls in the cockpit! Even the pilots who are trained and skilled to do so must possess a healthy fear of all the unknowns that are part of any given flight.

You know that common saying, "The more you know, the more you know what you don't know"? Think about an area of expertise you've developed, whether in school or work or life experience. The more knowledge you gain in that area, the more you realize how unfathomable the depths of that subject are, be it quantum physics, the mating rituals of songbirds, or infectious diseases.

Most of us understand that we can never know all there is to know about anything, even in areas in which we gain considerable experience and expertise. And yet we are meant to pursue truth, both understanding it and applying it. We must do so as though it is a great treasure that sits at the end of a long trail of stepping stones set within a flowing river. We can pursue that path only one stone at a time, ensuring as best we can that each stone is secure and that each place our foot lands will hold until we reach the next stone.

Truth is potent. It is a matter of life and death. It must be stewarded with care. You don't tell your toddler about the birds and the bees. Rather, you give facts and information slowly over time in age-appropriate doses. Similarly, employers, pastors, and counselors are entrusted every day with sensitive information that they need in order to do their jobs but that few others need or should have. God, too, has revealed himself over time, through his Word, through the incarnation, and through the inspiration of the Holy Spirit. He has yet to reveal it all. We cannot, in this earthly realm, see his full glory and live.

Emily Dickinson expresses this idea most eloquently and insightfully in one of my favorite poems:

> Tell all the truth but tell it slant—
> Success in Circuit lies
> Too bright for our infirm Delight
> The Truth's superb surprise
>
> As Lightning to the Children eased
> With explanation kind
> The Truth must dazzle gradually
> Or every man be blind—[10]

Truth is so bright that we cannot gaze at it directly. It would be like looking into the sun. We can manage just a slant of light. Like children afraid of a storm, we need only as much knowledge as we can understand. Such an explanation is the kindest. "The Truth must dazzle gradually," lest we be blinded by it. Or be felled at once by taking and eating forbidden fruit.

It was not the knowledge that was made available from the tree in Eden that was forbidden to Adam and Eve. It was the way in which that knowledge was gained that was wrong. Indeed, a better translation of the name of that tree—"the tree of knowing good and bad"—makes this point clearer, according to BibleProject. As creatures made in God's image, Adam and Eve were made with a moral capacity and given the role of stewarding the rest of creation. Surely, as Adam and Eve would have exercised both their moral sense and their God-given responsibility, God would have revealed to them over time the necessary knowledge of good and bad—the truth. Instead, they sought to know in their own way and on their own terms. That is how death entered the world. That's why, in translating the name as "the tree of knowing" rather than the more common "the tree of knowledge," the emphasis is put more properly not on *what* Adam and Eve came to learn but *how* they did it. They did not wait for God to reveal truth to them in his time and in his way.[11] "God not only knows everything, but he desires to teach us his ways"[12] and to do so *in his way*.

Finding and following your calling can require so much discernment and time that it's easy to try to grab the unripe apple off the tree rather than wait and work toward the proper time of harvest. We *are* made to know the truth. It will set us free. Likewise, we are made to know and fulfill our calling. But gaining such knowledge rightly takes time.

Much of that time involves getting to know yourself. Who you are. And who you aren't.

An illuminating picture of what can happen when we fail to know who we are is painted by Arthur Miller in the play *Death of a Salesman*.

Willy Loman, the salesman of the title, didn't know who he was. That was his tragedy.

The aging, ineffectual, lost Willy Loman has, we see at the start of the play, lived his life according to the mantras of his day—mid-twentieth-century America. Rather than being told, "Pursue your passion" (today's mantra), Willy has been told (and believes), "Be liked and you will never want."[13] Being well-liked is the formula Willy thinks will bring him and his two sons success and happiness. Early in life Willy sees the tremendous influence and popularity of an older salesman, and he spends his life trying to imitate this man. He fails to achieve the same success, however, because no one can ever succeed by trying to live someone else's life.

After Willy's death, his son Biff, looking at the work on the house Willy had done over the years, realizes that it was working with his hands that brought Willy the most joy. But Willy had looked down on that kind of work, believing a false narrative about what success must look like within the context of the American Dream. "He had all the wrong dreams. All, all wrong, he never knew who he was," Biff realizes.[14]

Willy held wrongheaded beliefs originating from the kind of folk advice that gets handed down by family and society, that has some truth but is bound to fail because its truth is assumed rather than examined. Willy's desire to be well-liked wasn't entirely wrong. We all want to be loved. But Willy got something else wrong. He thought being well-liked was the means to material and social success, and he thought such success would, in turn, make him well-liked. He made someone else's life his dream and, in so doing, failed to know himself. He would have been happier working with his hands, but he denied his own good gifts and desires for those of someone else. That is the tragedy. As Os Guinness says in *The Call*, "To understand ourselves, we need to know not only our gifts but also the deepest desires we long to fulfill."[15]

For a long time, I, like so many others in American society, wanted to own a home without even considering why. I assumed it was a sign of success. But it took my husband and me a long time to buy our first home (and we are not millennials!). I was close to completing a PhD, my husband was fulfilling his dream of playing music full-time, and we had a strong, healthy marriage and a loving church family. Why were those things not enough to count as "success"? Because I had another story in my head, one I had to replace with a truer one. (We did eventually buy our first home, and that turned out to be a nightmare. We have our dream home now, but it took many years and a lot of work.)

We can find our calling only by knowing the truth about ourselves—our strengths, our limitations, our passions, our potential. Knowing these things doesn't mean we will attain them. But knowing them can offer guidance and guardrails to keep us going in a truer direction. Often the desires we think are our own come from elsewhere. "The goal of vocation," Kathleen Cahalan writes, "is to find and live out of God's truth, a truth that takes on particularity in your life—the truth of who you are and how you live."[16]

The True

When we are making decisions about work and calling, we need to know not only ourselves but also the nature of our work itself.

I was lucky enough to learn one of these lessons early on during my college internship. When I decided in my sophomore year to change my major to English, I was uncertain enough about where that field of study would take me that I wanted to be practical, too, so I chose to minor in public relations and communication. (Remember earlier when I said that I often advise parents of college students that it's not always practical to be practical? I learned that lesson from my own life.) The public relations and communication minor entailed business courses (I still can't believe I took business courses!) and an internship, one I fulfilled by working at a marketing agency. That proved to be one of the most valuable experiences of my early working life. It was there, in a downtown building with giant windows looking out at the interstate that snaked alongside the riverfront while I toiled away in a cubicle, that I learned how much I despise office life, business attire, and a nine-to-five schedule. I don't know what else I thought it would be. But I had to experience this kind of work to find out what it was really like. After that, I decided to apply to graduate school to pursue an academic life. I never wore pantyhose again.

Of course, many, many people have to hold jobs doing work that they don't love. That is simply a given for most of those who have ever lived on planet Earth. The point is that when you *do* have the freedom and opportunity to choose your work and you are facing such decisions, knowing the nature of the work itself is essential to finding your vocation in truth. Finding your rightful calling means knowing the truth about yourself and the truth about your work. No one is served when someone does work they can't do well, even if they have the best intentions.

Dorothy Sayers doesn't mince words on this point: "No piety in the worker will compensate for work that is not true to itself; for any work that is untrue to its own technique is a living lie. . . . Work must be good work before it can call itself God's work."[17]

When I hear someone say that some modern work of art looks simple and easy to do, I tend to ask, "Do you know how to stretch a canvas and use acrylic paint?" Even handling the materials for making a painting requires knowledge I know I don't have. Just because something looks easy doesn't mean there aren't skills involved that we can't see on the surface. Truth about work requires acknowledging that there is much we don't know how to do that others, with hard work, have learned to do.

We need to know the truth about ourselves, the truth about the work, and finally, the truth about the needs of the world. Remember Don Quixote? He wanted so badly to be a knight in shining armor, imagining that the world needed him to be that. But that world was passing away. His romanticism prevented him from recognizing reality. There's an old idiom about going the way of the buggy whip. When we entered the age of the automobile, buggy whip makers were no longer in demand. Most of us aren't making vocational decisions as illusory as this, but it's crucial to remember that our calling in a particular time and place does depend in part on the reality of the world in our time.

For Christians, truth is so important and obvious that it almost goes without saying. And that's part of the problem. We believe so fiercely in the importance of truth and pursue it so relentlessly (or we think we do) that it's easy to assume that we are walking in truth as we think about calling.

Of course, truth includes honesty and integrity. It includes pursuing knowledge and growing in the skills related to the work we are doing. But Truth—with a capital T—encompasses much more than this.

We know that Jesus is the Truth. We know we are to walk with Jesus. We know we are not to do what his Word teaches us not to do. God isn't going to call you to be a prostitute. Got it. He's not going to call you to sell illegal drugs at the elementary school in your neighborhood. Check. He's not going to call you to run a website for folks who are "married but looking." For sure! He's not going to call people to do a lot of things people do in this world, because he never calls us to disobey him.

Yet, when you consider the deep and wide span of human history and the abundance and generative creativity that God has built into the world and the way it runs, it's easy to see that what God has placed off-limits is minuscule in comparison to the nearly infinite ways in which his design allows us to serve him by serving our neighbors.

Part of finding your calling in truth is acknowledging and accepting your limitations, just as much as you acknowledge and accept your gifts and strengths. No one can do or be everything. Yet how often do we find those with clear callings in one area proudly, defiantly, misguidedly, or foolishly stepping into other callings? Of course, it's easy to make such a mistake. (Willy Loman was misguided more than anything else. He wasn't trying to be a failure.) But sometimes I think we try to do too much or overstep our bounds because we live in a culture that believes the lie that we can do anything—and everything. You don't have to look hard to find examples of people who do so with aplomb. Or so it seems.

It's easy to look at someone's work—work that, because it's the fruit of years of labor, study, and practice, looks effortless—and think, "Wow, I want to do that too!" without considering those years of labor, study, and practice. (It's also easy to look at people who have found success without much labor and want that too. This might be a bigger problem.) But seeing something and wanting it is different from being called to do that thing.

I wanted to be a mother. But God didn't call me to that, even after treatment and surgery to free the line for his call. So, while some of you were creating and raising new bearers of God's image, I put my time into attending school, reading books, writing papers, translating *Beowulf*, teaching classes, reading more books, and then writing my own. (Okay, I have also spent some of that time tweeting.) The point is that no one gets to have it all. All we need—and all we should want—is what God calls us to. The situation he has assigned (1 Cor. 7:17) is good.

Our sense of reality and our expectations can be built by what we see around us. Human beings are by nature built for community and shaped by our communities. Our desires, as we saw earlier (in the story told by Blackaby about his son and the bicycle), are cultivated by the world around us.

That reality is magnified even more by the multiplicity of images and virtual communities offered to us by social media. Through the power of social media, we are offered an array of platters serving up various dishes, and we are left salivating over morsels we otherwise would not have known even existed.

With opportunities numbering near infinity, we must use wisdom and discernment in considering whether or not an opportunity is a call. Within the context of calling, what is really truth (what lines up squarely with reality) and what is a distortion of truth can be subtle and difficult to discern. But that's exactly why pursuing truth first can help you find your calling.

The Good

Goodness is truth made manifest. Just as truth is connected to knowing, goodness is connected to doing and how that doing is done.

We see this reality in God's dynamic acts of creation, which began at the foundation of the world as told in Genesis and continue in our lives today. God declared his acts of creation "good" and "very good."

This declaration of goodness is true, and it also points to beauty. Again, nothing can be good that is not also true and beautiful. Indeed, the word for "good," which God used to describe his creation, refers to both moral goodness and aesthetic goodness (beauty).[1]

This dual sense of the word "good" is still reflected today when, for example, we respond with "It was good" on being asked what we thought of a recent movie or concert. We might offer further nuance and clarification, but when we say something is good, we usually mean it was good in all the important ways.

The goodness we see in the world, even in its fallen state, is good because God made the world good. The good works we are able to do, even in our fallen human condition, are good only because they reflect his goodness. "We are God's handiwork, created in Christ Jesus to do good works" (Eph. 2:10). Our good works and good lives give glory to God (Matt. 5:16; 1 Pet. 2:12). Though this world is marked by unspeakable suffering and sin, it is filled with goodness, too, because God is good.

As the poet Gerard Manley Hopkins puts it in one of his most famous poems, "The world is charged with the grandeur of God."[2] The good life is one that sees and celebrates the fullness of the earth and its infinite goodness—and contributes to that goodness. This is the very purpose of your calling.

Of course, unlike God, we exist in time, and good things—including the good fruit of our labor—require time. We do not simply speak something into existence and POOF! it is there. As one writer says,

> Bread-making takes time, another created reality that communicates to us about God's glory. It takes time for a grain of wheat to die in the ground and then to grow. It takes time to harvest. It takes time for the yeast to work. It takes time to mix ingredients. It takes time to bake them. And all that time is good.[3]

Yes, it is *good*.

While gifts might be natural to a person, character takes time to develop. But as Diane Langberg points out, often "we confuse gifts with character."[4] Such confusion is to our detriment. It's human to want things quickly, right now. But there is no sidestepping the fact that the test of character, like the harvest of the fields, takes time.

Regardless of your work or calling, approaching it like a craft that can be mastered only after you submit to that work offers a different way of understanding calling than one based on mere passion alone. Cal Newport elaborates on this idea by contrasting the "craftsman mindset" with the "passion mindset," writing, "Whereas the craftsman mindset focuses on *what you can offer the world*, the passion mindset focuses instead on *what the world can offer you*. This mindset is how most people approach their working lives."[5] In our approach to work, the Christian, more than anyone, ought to want to offer something to the world rather than take something from it. But I'll be honest, I seldom hear someone say they "just want to serve" by using their gifts in such and such a place without hearing a hint of their wanting something for themselves in that service, whether that be recognition, influence, honor, or security. This is normal and human, of course. But there is a temptation, specific to the Christian context, to hide our own desires from ourselves behind the cloak of humble, selfless Christian service.

Newport will have none of that. *How* we work is more important than what the work is. "Working right trumps finding the right work," he says.[6]

As stewards of God's creation and cocreators with him of new creations, working right means acknowledging that we are using his materials and expressing his character and nature through our work, by our service, and in our callings. Wendell Berry offers bold words about this:

> Good human work honors God's work. Good work uses no thing without respect, both for what it is in itself and for its origin. It uses neither tool nor material that it does not respect and that it does not love. It honors nature as a great mystery and power, as an indispensable teacher, and as the inescapable judge of all work of human hands. It does not dissociate life and work, or pleasure and work, or love and work, or usefulness and beauty. To work without pleasure or affection, to make a product that is not both useful and beautiful, is to dishonor God, nature, the thing that is made, and whomever it is made for. This is blasphemy: to make shoddy work of the work of God. But such blasphemy is not possible when the entire Creation is understood as holy and when the works of God are understood as embodying and thus revealing His spirit.[7]

In an essay that is, strictly speaking, about work but is also helpful in thinking about calling more generally, Dorothy Sayers has much to say that is worth quoting.

First, calling, like work, is not just about income:

> The habit of thinking about work as something one does to make money is so ingrained in us that we can scarcely imagine what a revolutionary change it would be to think about it instead in terms of the work done. To do so would mean taking the attitude of mind we reserve for our unpaid work—our hobbies, our leisure interests, the things we make and do for

pleasure—and making that the standard of all our judgments about things and people. We should ask of an enterprise, not "will it pay?" but "is it good?"[8]

Second, the goodness of work resides, in part, in the goodness of what the work makes:

> And, whether by strange coincidence, or whether because of some universal law, as soon as nothing is demanded of the thing made but its own integral perfection, its own absolute value, the skill and labor of the worker are fully employed and likewise acquire an absolute value.[9]

To illustrate this point, Sayers argues,

> The Church's approach to an intelligent carpenter is usually confined to exhorting him not to be drunk and disorderly in his leisure hours, and to come to church on Sundays. What the Church should be telling him is this: that the very first demand that his religion makes upon him is that he should make good tables. . . . A building must be good architecture before it can be a good church.[10]

With words that speak sharply, particularly today, within an institutional church climate run too often by friend networks and nepotism, Sayers states, "God is not served by technical incompetence; and incompetence and untruth always result when the secular vocation is treated as a thing alien to religion."[11]

In sum, Sayers's argument is this: "The only Christian work is good work well done."[12]

The Good

Don't confuse good work done well with perfectionism. Indeed, quite the opposite.

You've probably heard some version of the truism that "the best is the enemy of the good," a saying that has appeared in various forms throughout history but was perhaps made most famous by the eighteenth-century French philosopher Voltaire. To demand nothing short of perfection is to end up with, well, nothing. And that's not at all good.

This fear of being less than perfect can be paralyzing for many, especially when facing life decisions such as discerning your vocation. One form of paralysis that plagues the modern church is rooted in the unbiblical language of "God's perfect plan" for your life. The good news is that God has no such perfect plan for your life! There is no blueprint that includes what job you should have, whom you should marry, and where you should live. So you can do away with all the anxiety about any accidental missteps away from God's road map for your life.

The fact that God does not have a detailed blueprint for our lives that we must follow to be in his perfect will is laid out thoroughly and biblically by Garry Friesen in *Decision Making and the Will of God*. Rather than encouraging us to seek the "perfect will of God" for our lives, which doesn't exist, Friesen exhorts us to use wisdom in making decisions.[13] The exercise of wisdom, Friesen argues, is the biblical approach, especially with respect to circumstances not addressed by the Bible. Such circumstances include our jobs and our vocations. The decision about your vocation, Friesen explains, "is *regulated* and affected by the moral will of God, but *not determined* by it."[14]

Coming from a completely different vantage point, Cal Newport confirms Friesen's wisdom in his own work journey. When he had to choose between going to MIT or Microsoft after college, Newport didn't become "paralyzed" the way many of his classmates would have, he says. Rather, he saw both options as ones that "would yield numerous opportunities that could be leveraged into a remarkable life."[15] He understood that he couldn't lose either way. What freedom there is in such an outlook!

For the Christian, this understanding comes with even more freedom. "God is working through what we do in vocation," Gene Edward Veith explains. "We are merely his instruments. When we realize that, we can relax."[16] We don't have to know what the "perfect" decision is because there isn't one. Truth is wider and deeper and more abundant than perfection. Truth has latitude for you as you feel your way toward calling—being as wise as you can, seeking counsel where you can, and being humble enough to adjust as needed along the way. As Proverbs 16:9 says, you can plan your way knowing that the Lord will direct your steps.

Goodness is both an end (a goal or destination) and a means (a manner or way of going). Goodness—the good life, the abundant life—is your telos, your purpose, your call.

Yet so much can tempt us away from that call.

For example, we are regularly inundated with images of thrilling careers, adventurous jobs, and dangerous occupations, all made to look even more exciting by the cable shows and social media reels that portray them in their most glamorous light. These larger-than-life models of work overshadow the types of jobs we are more likely to encounter every day, work that fulfills everyday needs: from the grocery store clerk to the coffee shop barista, from the power line worker to the train conductor, from the receptionist to the school janitor.

In *Deep Work*, Cal Newport reminds us,

> Throughout most of human history, to be a blacksmith or a wheelwright wasn't glamorous. But this doesn't matter, as the specifics of the work are irrelevant. The meaning uncovered by such efforts is due to the skill and appreciation inherent in craftsmanship—not the outcomes of their work.[17]

There is nothing at all wrong with the kind of work that ends up featured in multiple seasons on a streaming service, of course. But it's interesting to consider the contrasting advice of the apostle Paul when he encourages believers "to make it your ambition to lead a quiet life: You should mind your own business and work with your hands, just as we told you, so that your daily life may win the respect of outsiders and so that you will not be dependent on anybody" (1 Thess. 4:11–12).

What Paul is describing here is simply the inherent value of good work done well. Good work done well is a witness to the world of God, whose partners we human beings are in caring for his creation. This way of life offers the freedom of contentment. As Gordon Smith puts it,

> God often calls people to the obscure, the ordinary and the mundane. Some of the most important work that God accomplishes in the world is fulfilled by ordinary people doing ordinary work. This is not and cannot be merely tolerated, but rather is something we must embrace and even celebrate.[18]

Katie Andraski went to school and then worked in Christian institutions where it was ingrained in her to seek a vision of glory and to wield great influence, which she was expected to accomplish by publishing a book. That's not what happened. Instead, she spent thirty years writing *The River Caught Sunlight* before self-publishing it. But, Katie says, those years spent revising her novel "dumped me into a peace I haven't been able to shake. This was better for my soul than being published." She believes now "that maybe being small and hidden is closer to what God has in mind when we are told to follow Jesus who emptied himself, taking on the form of a servant." She says she feels "like a pastor to a small country church with my small readership and am grateful to be read." She has also taken much joy over the years in her horses and farm life.[19]

A more dramatic illustration of arriving at such a place of contentment is portrayed in the rollicking tale *Candide, or Optimism*, published in 1759 by Voltaire. This work satirizes a school of thought popular in the eighteenth century called philosophical optimism. This philosophy argued that because God, who is perfect, created this world, it must necessarily therefore be the best of all possible worlds. Many, like Voltaire—looking at the human suffering all around—disagreed. (Questions about the problem of evil have always existed, taking different forms and labels from age to age.) *Candide* was Voltaire's counterargument.

What unfolds in the narrative is a series of adventures centered on the title character, Candide. The worst possible things that could ever happen do happen to him and his companions, over and over and over. Candide stubbornly clings to his cheery idealism through it all until the very end. Having endured one catastrophe after another, one unhappiness after another, Candide finally comes to a new view of life. Settling on a small farm in the country with his remaining loved ones, Candide says there is only one thing they can do in this life where so much can go wrong: "We must cultivate our garden." One of his friends agrees. "Let us work," he says, "without speculating; it is the only way of rendering life tolerable."[20]

Admittedly, in striving to temper an overly optimistic view, Voltaire may have offered too pessimistic a view in its stead. The tale presents neither a sound explanation for the existence of evil nor a robust theology of work. Voltaire's religious views were complicated, to be sure, and he was a resounding critic of Christianity. Nevertheless, to read this tale and encounter its abrupt, simple ending is not only memorable but challenging in a good way. After all the over-the-top high jinks and calamities are said and done, in the end, the characters make for themselves quiet, peaceful lives rooted in companionship, faithfulness, and the good work of tending the land.

Perhaps *Candide* is a cheeky predecessor to Wendell Berry. Berry holds an earnest Christian belief, whereas Voltaire was ever the cynic. Nevertheless, each in his own way arrives at a picture of tilling the earth as a way to achieve a good life in this fallen world. Here is Berry's version of this view in "A Vision":

> If we will have the wisdom to survive,
> to stand like slow-growing trees
> on a ruined place, renewing, enriching it,
> if we will make our seasons welcome here,
> asking not too much of earth or heaven,
> then a long time after we are dead
> the lives our lives prepare will live
> there, their houses strongly placed
> upon the valley sides, fields and gardens
> rich in the windows. The river will run
> clear, as we will never know it,
> and over it, birdsong like a canopy.
> On the levels of the hills will be
> green meadows, stock bells in noon shade.
> On the steeps where greed and ignorance cut down
> the old forest, an old forest will stand,
> its rich leaf-fall drifting on its roots.
> The veins of forgotten springs will have opened.
> Families will be singing in the fields.
> In their voices they will hear a music
> risen out of the ground. They will take
> nothing from the ground they will not return,

> whatever the grief at parting. Memory,
> native to this valley, will spread over it
> like a grove, and memory will grow
> into legend, legend into song, song
> into sacrament. The abundance of this place,
> the songs of its people and its birds,
> will be health and wisdom and indwelling
> light. This is no paradisal dream.
> Its hardship is its possibility.[21]

Voltaire rejects the idea that this is the best of all possible worlds. But Berry at least sees in the hardship—in the work—the possibility. And the goodness.

The Beautiful

Beauty calls.

Simply by being beautiful, the thing of beauty calls us to it, attracts us, draws us near.

The sunrise calls us. The sunset calls us. The mountaintop vista calls us. The aurora borealis calls us. The peony calls us. The dappled gray Arabian horse calls us. The sleek red Mustang convertible calls us. The impressionist painting calls us. The strikingly beautiful person calls us.

But these invoke only one sense of beauty: the physical. Thomas Aquinas defines this kind of beauty as something that, upon being seen, pleases.[1]

But there's a metaphorical sense of beauty that also calls us, draws us, and attracts us.

We enjoy a beautiful friendship. We appreciate a beautiful job done by a coworker. A family has a beautiful time at the beach. We are drawn to the person with a beautiful smile. Everyone loves the person with a beautiful spirit.

The movie *Barbie* has an unforgettable scene in which the stunningly gorgeous Barbie (played by Margot Robbie), who has journeyed out of Barbie world and into the real one, finds herself seated on a bench next to a quiet elderly woman whose face is marked by lines and age (played by Ann Roth, a ninety-one-year-old costume designer). Barbie stares at the woman in wonder, having never seen anyone like this in her world. Then, after a few moments, she says to the woman, "You're so beautiful." The woman, looking straight at Barbie with a little surprise and twinkling eyes, replies firmly, "I *know* it." And they both laugh.[2]

Such beauty is seen not only by the eyes but by the soul, and when seen (or noticed or understood), it pleases.

This beauty, too, beckons us.

The centrality of truth and goodness in the faithful Christian life is readily apparent. Indeed, orthodoxy (true doctrine) and orthopraxy (right practice) are the focus of most preaching, teaching, and discipleship. Beauty, on the other hand, often seems peripheral, unimportant, and optional, particularly within the modern world. Beauty can even be seen as excessive or dispensable in a world rife with so many other dire needs. But aesthetic experience is central to our very humanity, to the image of God in us. As Christians, we need to be as concerned about orthopathy (right feeling) as we are about orthodoxy and orthopraxy.[3]

The Greek word *kalon*, which carries the meaning of both "goodness" and "beauty," an ideal of beauty that is manifested both morally and physically, has etymological connections to the English word "call." This word and its variants occur multiple times in the New Testament. One illustrative example occurs in Matthew 12:33, which says, "Make a tree good [*kalon*] and its fruit will be good [*kalon*]." Such a tree and its fruit are good and beautiful in every way: physically, morally, and aesthetically. This Greek word suggests that it is not only physical beauty that calls us. Moral beauty (what is good) attracts us too. The wise teacher draws us in. The worker who cares about the quality and integrity of her work attracts our business. The kind neighbor is welcomed. The just man wins us over.

These examples show how hard it can be to distinguish beauty from goodness and truth. Beauty is the form, the outward showing. Ultimately, form and content can't be separated, although we can distinguish them in our thinking.

To understand the spiritual reality in a work of art or a work of nature is to discern truth. Beauty "incites in us a longing for truth," according to philosopher Elaine Scarry, because the very act of judging beauty causes us to consider the very ideas of certainty and error as we are confronted with the certainty (or error) in our judgment. "The beautiful, almost without any effort of our own," Scarry explains, "acquaints us with the mental event of conviction, and so pleasurable a mental state is this that ever afterwards one is willing to labor, struggle, wrestle with the world to locate enduring sources of conviction—to locate what is true."[4]

Have you ever watched a dog show and rooted for your favorite dog? In dog shows where different breeds of dogs are judged against one another for their beauty (as opposed to performance), each dog is judged for how its conformation (the physical form) holds up to the breed standard. The breed standard is developed to allow the dog to do what it was bred to do (its function). A beautiful pointer was bred to do something different from a beautiful Saint Bernard. The size, coat, and shape of each breed, from nose to ears to tail, help it better perform its job. The dog's form supports its function. Each breed is beautiful in its own way. (And mutts are beautiful in being mutts!)

Beauty's existence requires us all to be dog show judges—and, like any good judge, we seek to be certain in our judgments even while recognizing that we could be wrong. Whether or not we agree on what is beautiful or are able to achieve the standard in our work, the key, as Roger Scruton points out, is that we attempt it, that we know we ought to attempt to judge it and aim for it.[5]

Beauty reminds us in this way that right and wrong do exist. And not just in show dog rings.

Beauty calls, which serves as a reminder that beauty is foremost an aesthetic experience, something perceived bodily through our physical senses. Yet recognizing beauty as beauty occurs through the intellect, through reason.

While the modern use of the word "aesthetics" is usually applied narrowly to an object's visual appearance, the word's origins imply the subjective element of aesthetic experience. Consider that the word "anesthesia" has the same root word; its prefix denotes the blocking of physical sensation and sensory experience. You can't sense the beauty of music without first hearing it. You can't sense the beauty of a rainbow without first seeing it.

Even though aesthetic experience begins with the senses, it encompasses much more than mere physical sensation. All animals see and hear things, but only humans make rational meaning out of them. This meaning constitutes aesthetic experience and our understanding of beauty. Animals don't seem to perceive and appreciate beauty as we humans can. They see by the light cast by the sunrise, but they don't perceive the beauty it brings. They respond to a whistle, a clap, or even music, but they don't judge whether a song is in tune (although they may react in their animal nature to something exciting or unpleasant—my grandparents once had a Boston terrier that would jump up and down and bark at my grandfather's trombone when it was played, to everyone's great amusement).

An aesthetic experience is more than just a sensory experience. Rather than ending with a purely instinctive response to sensory experience, our heart, mind, and soul receive and interpret the phenomenon.

It's notable, too, that the literal meaning of "emotion" is "movement out of"—in other words, a "stirring" or "agitation"—and it later came to mean "feelings." We know from how addictions work that our emotions (our inner movements and stirrings) can be provoked by bad and ugly things (social media alerts, pornography, fear), as well as good things, and that our bodies can become habituated into seeking those bodily responses (especially dopamine hits) from the bad rather than the good.

At the most fundamental level, an aesthetic experience is an affective experience, one that moves us. While in the context of beauty we would be apt to understand the word "move" metaphorically (as in being *moved* by a song), the word should be understood literally as well: to be moved by something is to experience a bodily response, such as a quickened heartbeat, widened eyes, gathering tears, a gasp, a nod, a smile.

We are moved by what we desire (or by what we fear), and we desire what we love, as James K. A. Smith shows in his liturgical anthropology, a phrase that describes how habits have power over our spiritual formation.[6] Our loves and desires can be so shaped by ingrained habits that our aesthetic responses may not even be conscious.

Because our experience of beauty depends on our first perceiving and then recognizing the beauty before us, seeing the way we bring beauty into our daily work requires our attention and intention. When the term "aesthetics" was first coined in the eighteenth century, it emerged as a kind of "science" or knowing that comes through sensuous experience and the judgments that are part of artistic taste. This new field of philosophical inquiry examined the kind of knowing we gain from hearing a song, seeing a painting, reading a story, or watching a film—the part of the experience that can't be recreated by a summary or description. The taste and judgment required for aesthetic experience explains why some great works of art go unappreciated until we are ready for them, whether in terms of maturity or learning or life experience. I hear over and over from people who reencounter works of art they couldn't appreciate earlier in life that they can now. Such experiences merely reflect our intellectual, emotional, and spiritual growth that readies us for what was already and always there in the object of art.

Although classical conceptions of aesthetics would have it otherwise, perhaps beauty is, in this way, in the eye of the beholder. And if so, we need to make sure our eyes are healthy. In his book *Beauty: What It Is and Why It Matters*, John-Mark Miravalle writes that in order for things that have beauty (as opposed to those things that are not beautiful) to "inflame our passions," those passions must be "cultivated and ordered." Before beauty can motivate us toward virtue, we must exercise virtue by developing our ability to perceive and discern beauty.[7] To experience beauty is to perceive the goodness of something and take delight in it.[8] Thus, "through beauty we're able to trigger *physical* reactions to *spiritual* reality."[9]

Focusing more on the spiritual or intellectual than the physical can lead Christians to undervalue the role that sensory or aesthetic experience plays in our formation and understanding. But God does not disregard the physical or material. Indeed, it was God who ordained to bring salvation to humanity by taking on a bodily form in the person of Jesus Christ.

When the Bible speaks of the glory of God, it is speaking of his beauty. It is his magnificence made manifest. The glory of God refers to his significance or weightiness. His beautiful presence.[10] God's presence is manifested in the incarnation of Christ, just as it was manifested in the Old Testament in the fiery bush, the pillar of cloud, the consuming fire—and is manifested through his image bearers in the things we make and the work we do. With the coming of Christ, we can say with John that "we have seen his glory" (John 1:14). (This despite the fact that Jesus had no comeliness or physical beauty, as prophesied in Isa. 53:2.) The incarnation brought God to humankind in a physical form that could be seen, heard, smelled, and touched—and whose bodily death, burial, and resurrection we remember through the tasting of bread and wine, another aesthetic or sensory experience.

All the beauty in the world—whether that made by God or that made by those created in his image—beckons us to him. God created a beautiful world that displays visibly his invisible qualities, a world that calls us to him, so that we are without excuse (Rom. 1:20).

The blessings proclaimed by Christ in his Sermon on the Mount are called the "Beatitudes," a word that comes from the same Indo-European root for the word "beautiful."[11] Blessed—and beautiful—are the lives of those marked by meekness, mercy, mourning, peacefulness, purity, hunger for justice, and persecution for justice's sake. Most of these are attributes and conditions we would not seek, yet they serve as refining fires that burn away impurities to make precious metals shine.

But what is beauty? Can it really be defined? The modern world has fallen for the myth that "beauty is in the eye of the beholder," which, as noted above, is only partly true. There are objective qualities of beauty, even if these qualities might be debated or, even if agreed upon, require seasoned skills to discern or assess.

Thomas Aquinas famously identified the properties of beauty as *proportion*, *luminosity* (some translations render the underlying Latin word as "clarity" or "illumination"), and *integrity*.[12] (Here we have another set of three!)

If we apply these qualities to a work of visual art, such as a painting, we would look for a kind of balance in the scene that offers the right proportion (a common example of this is the composition principle known as the rule of thirds[13]), an appropriate amount and placement of light, and all that is necessary to make the picture seem complete (even what's left out creates the content of what's left in).

If we consider these qualities in a less physical or material context, as in a context of spiritual or moral beauty, then we can think about the qualities of proportion, luminosity, and integrity in corresponding ways.

Proportion alone invites various applications. As we've seen, we are all called to multiple vocations over our lives. We are called to family relationships, to citizenship, to being a neighbor and friend—and to the varying work we are called to do in different seasons. Proportionality requires us to offer the time, energy, and attention needed and appropriate to those callings at any given time. There will be times in life when family needs are greater, and your work will get minimal attention for a while. Speaking in general terms, I think the desire of younger generations today to focus more on quality of life (including doing more work from home) and less on climbing corporate or career ladders has helped shift the scales toward a more beautiful proportion. Even in seasons when plowing into work headlong is necessary and wise, that work will entail within it some components that require less attention, some more. The way I proportion my time when working on a book, for example, would not be good or beautiful for my entire life—but it is true to what is needed in the season.

Achieving luminosity in one's calling evokes a number of things. Even the word "luminosity" is interesting to think about. It suggests light, incandescence, glowing, enlightenment, clarity, illumination. Preachers bring luminosity to the Word by illuminating the text. Teachers bring clarity to students about otherwise difficult and mysterious subjects, and the best teachers also shine light on other subjects by pointing out connections. For those in public work such as politics or media, we might recall that old phrase about shedding more light than heat. One national newspaper's slogan—"Democracy Dies in Darkness"—gestures toward the light brought to bear in the world by the work of journalism (as does the title of the film *Spotlight*, depicting the role one newspaper played in exposing decades of horrific sexual abuse in the church). In less public callings, seeking and shining light might be understood in an infinite number of ways. I think, for example, of how my late mother frequently called online support centers, whether for her computer or banking or other tasks. You can hardly bless an eighty-eight-year-old lady more than in being pleasing and helpful over the phone when trying to help her navigate a technological issue. When such a person made her day, it made my day too. That person out there in the call center may never know it. Years ago, we hired an exterminator to help us with a persistent pest problem in the house. I will never forget the way his face beamed when he finally figured out a solution. His work was the kind few would want to do but many of us need, and it gave him great joy to do it well. His joy gave me joy. Similarly, a local meteorologist in our area is beloved by the community not only because of his excellence in predicting and explaining the weather but more so because of the enthusiastic way in which he provides frequent and detailed updates throughout the day. (We love you, George! Rain or shine, you are simply radiant.) Such people do their work with a luminosity that is simply beautiful. And how can we discuss luminosity without being reminded of the way some women who are with child simply glow?

Integrity carries the most obvious meaning. There are as many ways to have integrity in one's work as there are jobs. We obviously think of honesty and fairness when we think of integrity. But we can also think of wholeness. There are many ways to bring your whole self to your calling. I think, for example, of a colleague with whom I served as a fellow English professor for many years. She was a wife and mother before she was an English professor, and one of the greatest gifts she brought to her teaching was being motherly toward her students, whoever needed such mothering. Often that included football players who were taking English only because they had to, which didn't bother her at all. She just mothered them into the five-paragraph essay and short research paper. Even proper boundaries that are often needed between various roles and relationships are a way to maintain integrity within the various callings of life. For example, therapists are often wisely firm about not becoming social media friends with their clients, and most accountants prefer not to give tax advice at dinner parties. Well-drawn lines give integrity to a whole life and add to its beauty.

Beauty is by no means perfection. The Japanese word *wabi-sabi* refers to the kind of beauty that is found in subtle flaws. The word invokes an aesthetic and even a worldview that contrasts with the classical Greco-Roman standard that values consistency and idealizes perfection. The poet Gerard Manley Hopkins understood this kind of beauty and celebrated it in his poem "Pied Beauty." The word "pied," meaning "of two or more colors," goes against the classical understanding of beauty as uniformity in color and appearance. The poem describes a variety of things that have different colors, stippling, freckling, or other visually strange aspects about them. The poem is particularly relevant to the topic of calling, work, and vocation because it includes human efforts and tools as examples of the beauty to be found in imperfection:

> Glory be to God for dappled things—
>   For skies of couple-colour as a brinded cow;
>   For rose-moles all in stipple upon trout that swim;
> Fresh-firecoal chestnut-falls; finches' wings;
>   Landscape plotted and pieced—fold, fallow, and plough;
>   And áll trádes, their gear and tackle and trim.
>
> All things counter, original, spare, strange;
>   Whatever is fickle, freckled (who knows how?)
>   With swift, slow; sweet, sour; adazzle, dim;
> He fathers-forth whose beauty is past change:
>   Praise him.[14]

As with all of Hopkins's poetry, these things that are imperfect in color or aspect not only are beautiful in their own right but remind us of the uniform and unchanging God to whom all praise is due. He is the source, Hopkins knew, of eternal beauty.

Beauty, like the sun, has natural effects just in being what it is.

One of these natural effects of beauty is that in drawing us to itself, beauty draws our attention away from ourselves (even if only, alas, momentarily).

Philosopher Iris Murdoch describes the power of beauty—whether beauty created by God in nature or by human beings through art—to form and reform us through what she calls "unselfing." In drawing us away from ourselves, our own self-interest, and our subjectivity to the objective world around us, beauty helps us grow in virtue and goodness. In *The Sovereignty of Good*, Murdoch writes,

> Beauty is the convenient and traditional name of something which art and nature share, and which gives a fairly clear sense to the idea of quality of experience and change of consciousness. I am looking out of my window in an anxious and resentful state of mind, oblivious of my surroundings, brooding perhaps on some damage done to my prestige. Then suddenly I observe a hovering kestrel. In a moment everything is altered. The brooding self with its hurt vanity has disappeared. There

is nothing now but kestrel. And when I return to thinking of the other matter it seems less important. And of course, this is something which we may also do deliberately: give attention to nature in order to clear our minds of selfish care.[15]

Elaine Scarry calls this kind of response to beauty "radical decentering." In *On Beauty and Being Just*, she explains,

> At the moment we see something beautiful, we undergo a radical decentering.... It is not that we cease to stand at the center of the world, for we never stood there. It is that we cease to stand even at the center of our own world. We willingly cede our ground to the thing that stands before us.[16]

Beauty draws us out of ourselves and connects us to others because beauty is something we want to share with others. Beauty cultivates unselfing. "Look at the sky," we say to a loved one when the light forms a certain way. "Do you see the moon right now?" a friend who lives a couple of hours away will text. "See what I made?" beams a child who has drawn a figure with crayon on paper. Even if we have escaped to a mountain trail for some much-needed solitude, most of us likely will later share something of the beauty we heard, saw, or felt there.

Maggie Smith's "Poem Beginning with a Retweet" puts the point even more profoundly and poignantly. The poem begins by quoting a post Smith saw on X:

> *If you drive past horses and don't say horses*
> *you're a psychopath.*[17]

The poem goes on to describe the many kinds of things—a bird, a butterfly, a fin, a shell, the moon—that ought to make us want to show them to everyone around us. If we don't, the poem suggests, we risk losing our very selves because in turning toward beauty and sharing it with others we prevent ourselves from "receding" until we are "gone." The one who loses their life finds it.

It is in this turning away from ourselves to the thing of beauty, then perhaps to someone (or Someone) else, that we encounter the way in which beauty is fruitful. Whether physically, spiritually, or morally, beauty is generative. It is creative.

Scarry says that beauty invites, even demands, replication. "Beauty brings copies of itself into being."[18] Beauty might be recreated through drawing a picture of the beautiful object. It might be recreated by writing an essay on the beautiful work. It might be recreated by conceiving or begetting a child, she explains.[19]

The desire to make a copy is the pull toward immortality and eternity.

To pursue beauty in our callings is, in part, to pursue the generative (and generous) aspect of beauty. As Scarry says, the one who perceives beauty "is led to a more capacious regard for the world."[20] After all, as we've already seen, calling is about serving our neighbors. Such serving is, like beauty, fruitful.

Capacious.

With attention and intention, we can strive to make even more beauty through our callings. Perhaps that means mentoring others (or being mentored) in what you do. Or making some of your work available to those who might not otherwise afford or have access to it as a kind of offering to the world. Or it might be merely recognizing and appreciating what is already generative in your work.

You may be weary of teaching your toddler how to tie his shoe (it would be easier just to do it yourself, after all). But teaching the skill so he can do it himself is more generative than doing it yourself.

You may wish the podcast you are hosting with your best friend from college were getting more likes and shares—like that show hosted by the bearded guy that goes viral weekly on every social media platform. But the seeds of truth and wisdom you plant in the souls of your listeners will likely bear good fruit long after the weekly hot takes have burned out.

If beauty is that which upon being seen pleases, then you might assume that the more you are "seen" the more beautiful you are. But beauty is a quality not a quantity.

I have a dear friend who couldn't punctuate a sentence if her life depended on it. I've helped her numerous times over the years when she needed something written that needed to be right. The first time my friend, who is a professional gardener and florist, came to my house to help me with my fledgling flower gardens, she made me pull out a lot that was detracting from the beauty. "Think of it as writing paragraphs," she said. "You have to cut and cut and move a lot of things around." Sure enough, her work helped my flowers breathe, blossom, and bloom. She helped me generate more beauty.

Beauty, in order to *be* beautiful, must be bound and framed, put together like an essay, like a flower garden, like shoelaces, like thoughtful words. Such boundaries can be formed by nature—as in the natural rhythms of the seasons or the raging forest fires that allow the earth to renew itself—or through human effort—as when a picture includes in the frame only what makes the scene beautiful. A garden marries art and nature. And this "attempt to match our surroundings to ourselves and ourselves to our surroundings is arguably a human universal."[21]

Order, not chaos, is beauty.

John-Mark Miravalle describes beauty as a harmony between order and wonder, between pattern and newness, between perfection and surprise. Referring to the character Innocent Smith in G. K. Chesterton's *Manalive*, Miravalle illuminates the way such an understanding of beauty can be applied to the way we live (which would, of course, include the way we work and fulfill our callings): "Break the conventions; keep the commandments."[22]

Scarry connects beauty to the commandments by arguing for beauty's connection to justice. She points out that another word for "beauty" is "fair," which also means "just." One definition of fairness is symmetry within relationships.[23] Beauty is itself a call for such symmetry.

Symmetry in various callings might look like the most vulnerable member of a family—an infant, for example—receiving more caregiving from other members of the family, a balance that shifts as that child matures. Many years later, that symmetry may reverse once the child who is well grown begins to care for the parents as age confers on them increasing vulnerability. Symmetry for the elected official requires her to represent faithfully and well the members of the community she serves. Symmetry for the public servant who protects the lives and well-being of others, putting his own life and well-being at risk every day, requires good pay, respect, and care from those he protects. Symmetry for the Good Shepherd means leaving the ninety-nine who are tucked safely into the fold to go out in search of the one that is lost, for it is just, fair, and fit to do so.

Beauty fulfills what Scruton calls fittingness. Fittingness, Scruton says, describes a properly hung door, a beautifully arranged garden, a properly set table, and even a solution "to a problem that can be solved in more than one way."[24]

One of my favorite accounts to follow on X belongs to a menswear writer who posts examples of well-dressed and not-so-well-dressed men. The difference between the two almost always comes down to fit. Even more than color, style, or material (although these do matter), clothing looks best when it fits the person properly. One suit on one man looks divine, on another, disastrous.

And sure enough, the women's clothing that the algorithms advertise to me—clothing that drapes so beautifully on tall, lanky models—will never fit like that on short, stocky me. That is a truth I have to live with.

Unfortunately, we live in a world where most ideals of fittingness don't fit most real people, literally or metaphorically.

But we can keep seeking that which truly does fit us.

Fittingness is our attempt to make order in the world and to feel at home in it.[25] It is the same work done by Adam and

Eve both in the garden and out of it. It is the work done behind the pulpit and in front of it. It is the work done in the home and outside it. It is the work done in the church and in the world. It is the good work done by the carpenter, the whittler, the ice skater, the film director, the farrier, the dog trainer, the truck driver, the window installer, the grocery clerk, the musician, the teacher, the writer, the artist, the stenographer, the hospice nurse, the journalist, the city slicker, the country dweller, the suburbanite, the mother, the father, the daughter, the son, and the friend.

Walt Whitman depicts the beauty of all kinds of work, roles, and callings in his poem "I Hear America Singing":

> I hear America singing, the varied carols I hear,
> Those of mechanics, each one singing his as it should
>   be blithe and strong,
> The carpenter singing his as he measures his plank
>   or beam,
> The mason singing his as he makes ready for work,
>   or leaves off work,
> The boatman singing what belongs to him in his boat,
>   the deckhand singing on the steamboat deck,
> The shoemaker singing as he sits on his bench, the
>   hatter singing as he stands,
> The wood-cutter's song, the ploughboy's on his way
>   in the morning, or at noon intermission or at
>   sundown,
> The delicious singing of the mother, or of the young
>   wife at work, or of the girl sewing or washing,

> Each singing what belongs to him or her and to none else,
> The day what belongs to the day—at night the party of young fellows, robust, friendly,
> Singing with open mouths their strong melodious songs.[26]

What is vocation but an answer to the universal call to match our surroundings to ourselves and ourselves to our surroundings? What is vocation but "each singing what belongs to him or her and to none else"? How can such a call not turn to singing when we harmonize ourselves with the world in which we find ourselves?

The thing about calling is that—even if the work isn't our driving passion, even if we embrace it reluctantly, even if we dream of another life (à la *The Midnight Library*)—there is, in the end, something about it that fits us.

Fittingness is glorious.

Whatever your calling is, you have been fitted for it.

Maybe as with a pair of favorite jeans or an old married couple, the fit will get better over time. But the fit matters. The right fit is always beautiful. Sometimes it takes a while to discover and grow into it. But somehow it happens along the way, along the journey in pursuit of the good, the true, and the beautiful.

Your true calling looks beautiful on you.

And in it (it's true) you will do the world—and yourself—so much good.

Acknowledgments

This book grew out of a talk I gave in 2021 at an event hosted by the Rabbit Room. My first thanks go to Andrew Peterson and all his rabbity comrades.

I'm extremely grateful to have worked again with the sharp and sharpening team at Brazos. Bob Hosack is not only an editor I trust and admire, but he has also become a friend. I can say the same of Jeremy Wells, who has now shepherded three book projects for me—from proposal to title to cover to the launch of the work out into the world. It has been a great joy to see breakfasts and dinners with Bob and Jeremy transform like magic into real books, including this one. Thank you, too, to Eric Salo, Paula Gibson, and Shelly MacNaughton for playing such key parts in the whole process and for fulfilling those roles so well. I'm so glad you were called to work with me.

Thank you to those who allowed me to share bits of their stories and some of their words in this book: Katie Andraski,

Chris Davis, Myndi Lawrence, David Rowe, Sarah Sanderson, Julie Anne Smith, and Jennifer Wiseman.

I am thankful to Sarah Michael Henry who so ably handles my scheduling and correspondence and, by keeping my calendar straight, keeps my mind straight too.

Whitney Meintjes, whom I met at a talk I gave while the book was still in progress, served as an insightful, enthusiastic, and, most importantly, honest reader of the manuscript. Her feedback during the drafting process was invaluable, and I'm grateful for her time and investment not only in this book but in the very idea of calling. They say writers should have the names and faces of real people in their minds when they write in order to address a real audience. Thank you, Whit, for being a flesh-and-bones reader by answering my call to be one.

If there is anyone I can look at in my life right now to see the phenomenon of vocation as both a providence and a mystery, that person is Meridith Tugwell. When I left my academic post—along with all its perks and benefits—Meridith stepped up as my volunteer research assistant, getting in return only my deepest thanks. Meridith allows me to get far more done than I otherwise could. I don't deserve such grace, but I gratefully receive the gift.

Finally, I can't imagine how my life would have turned out if I had not been called to be Roy's wife, and he my husband. I am sure this book would never have been written because I would not have lived the life I have without him. And I wouldn't want any other.

Notes

Questions

1. I say a lot more about the way of Jesus in my book *The Evangelical Imagination: How Stories, Images, and Metaphors Created a Culture in Crisis* (Brazos, 2023).

Work

1. Or "folded in," as the case may be (as any fans of *Schitt's Creek* know).
2. What an insightful commentary this offers on human systems based on slave labor. Not only does chattel slavery degrade human dignity, but it is premised on a depraved and unbiblical view of work.
3. John Mark Comer, *Garden City: Work, Rest, and the Art of Being Human* (Zondervan, 2015), 37–39.
4. John Milton, *Paradise Lost* 4.437–48, in *The Riverside Milton*, ed. Roy Flannagan (Houghton Mifflin, 1998), 455 (spelling and capitalization slightly modified by me to modernize).
5. Milton, *Paradise Lost* 9.205–12, in Flannagan, *Riverside Milton*, 590.
6. Robert Hayden, "Those Winter Sundays," in *Collected Poems of Robert Hayden*, ed. Frederick Glaysher (Liveright, 1985), available at https://www.poetryfoundation.org/poems/46461/those-winter-sundays.
7. Ben Witherington III, *Work: A Kingdom Perspective on Labor* (Eerdmans, 2011), xii–xv.
8. Emily Dickinson, "What Is—'Paradise,'" in *The Complete Poems of Emily Dickinson*, ed. Thomas H. Johnson (Back Bay Books, 1961), 99.

9. Gordon T. Smith, *Courage and Calling: Embracing Your God-Given Potential*, rev. ed. (IVP Books, 2011), 32.

10. Dominick S. Hernández, *Proverbs: Pathways to Wisdom* (Abingdon, 2020), 130.

11. Dorothy L. Sayers, *Why Work?* (CreateSpace, 2014), 17.

12. Madeleine L'Engle, *And It Was Good: Reflections on Beginnings* (Harold Shaw, 1983), 19.

13. George Herbert, "The Elixir," available at Poetry Foundation, accessed December 2, 2024, https://www.poetryfoundation.org/poems/44362/the-elixir.

14. Whether or not *Moll Flanders* is a novel or a precursor to the novel is a much-debated literary question.

15. Daniel Defoe, *Moll Flanders* (1722; repr., Dover, 1996), 140, 147, 142, 144, 154, 174.

16. Os Guinness, *The Call: Finding and Fulfilling God's Purpose for Your Life*, 20th anniv. ed. (W, 2018), 181–82.

17. Guinness, *The Call*, 71.

18. Guinness, *The Call*, 72.

19. Guinness, *The Call*, 225.

Passion

1. Cal Newport, *So Good They Can't Ignore You: Why Skills Trump Passion in the Quest for Work You Love* (Little, Brown, 2012), ix.

2. Newport, *So Good They Can't Ignore You*, 16–17.

3. Steve Rose, "What Does It Mean to Follow Your Passion?," Steve RosePhD.com, accessed August 21, 2024, https://steverosephd.com/what-does-it-mean-to-follow-your-passion.

4. Sarah Sanderson, email message to author, March 10, 2024. Shared with permission.

5. Kate Kennedy, *One in a Millennial: On Friendship, Feelings, Fangirls, and Fitting In* (St. Martin's, 2023), 235–36.

6. Rose, "What Does It Mean to Follow Your Passion?"

7. Henry Blackaby, Richard Blackaby, and Claude King, *Experiencing God*, rev. and exp. ed. (Lifeway, 2007), 109.

8. Jane Austen, *Sense and Sensibility* (B&H, 2020), 263.

9. Austin Kleon, *Steal like an Artist: Ten Things Nobody Told You about Being Creative* (Workman, 2012), 68.

10. Newport, *So Good They Can't Ignore You*, 14–15.

11. Newport, *So Good They Can't Ignore You*, xviii.

12. Newport, *So Good They Can't Ignore You*, 12.

13. Newport, *So Good They Can't Ignore You*, 22.

14. Samantha Klassen, *The Threads of Vocation: A Comic* (Saint Benedict's Table and Collegeville Institute, 2021), available at https://medium.com/@samanthaklassen124/the-threads-of-vocation-a-comic-39bd8b8ad22f.

15. Jon Schlosberg, Lindsey Griswold, Haley Yamada, Janice McDonald, and Steve Osunsami, "America's Nun Population in Steep Decline," ABC News, July 27, 2022, https://abcnews.go.com/US/americas-nun-population-steep-decline/story?id=87426990.

16. Frederick Douglass, *Narrative of the Life of Frederick Douglass, an American Slave, Written by Himself*, ed. William L. Andrews and William S. McFeely (Norton, 2017), 30.

17. Thomas Gray, "Elegy Written in a Country Churchyard," in *Norton Anthology of English Literature: The Major Authors*, ed. Stephen Greenblatt, 9th ed. (Norton, 2013), 1366–1400.

18. Os Guinness, *The Call: Finding and Fulfilling God's Purpose for Your Life*, 20th anniv. ed. (W, 2018), 77.

Definitions

1. "Elizabeth Gilbert on Distinguishing Between Hobbies, Jobs, Careers, & Vocation | Acumen Academy," posted June 19, 2017, by Acumen Academy, YouTube, 9 min., 43 sec., https://youtu.be/0g7ARarFNnw.

2. "Career," *Online Etymology Dictionary*, accessed December 2, 2024, https://www.etymonline.com/word/career#etymonline_v_5378.

3. Bryan J. Dik and Ryan D. Duffy, *Make Your Job a Calling: How the Psychology of Vocation Can Change Your Life at Work* (Templeton, 2012), 11.

Calling

1. Tony Martin, "Randall Wallace Shares His Thoughts on Music, Hollywood, and Faith," *Baptist Record*, November 21, 2023, https://thebaptistrecord.org/randall-wallace-shares-his-thoughts-on-music-hollywood-and-faith.

2. Kate Kennedy, *One in a Millennial: On Friendship, Feelings, Fangirls, and Fitting In* (St. Martin's, 2023), 88–89.

3. Os Guinness, *The Call: Finding and Fulfilling God's Purpose for Your Life*, 20th anniv. ed. (W, 2018), 61.

4. Gustaf Wingren, *Luther on Vocation*, trans. Carl C. Rasmussen (Wipf & Stock, 2004), 10.

5. "2024 SBC Pastors' Conference—Sunday Night," posted June 9, 2024, by Baptist Press, YouTube, 3 hr., 35 min., https://youtu.be/kfpVj4kXoKI.

6. Michael Berg, *Vocation: The Setting for Human Flourishing* (1517 Publishing, 2021), 32.

7. Gene Edward Veith, *God at Work: Your Christian Vocation in All of Life* (Crossway, 2002), 31, 33, 40.

8. Guinness, *The Call*, viii.

9. Viktor E. Frankl, *Man's Search for Meaning* (1946; repr., Beacon, 2006), xiv–xv.

10. Andrew Peterson, *Adorning the Dark: Thoughts on Community, Calling, and the Mystery of Making* (B&H, 2019), 44–45.

11. Peterson, *Adorning the Dark*, 47.

12. Bryan J. Dik and Ryan D. Duffy, *Make Your Job a Calling: How the Psychology of Vocation Can Change Your Life at Work* (Templeton, 2012), 3–4.

13. "Americans Love to Ask People 'What Do You Do?' It's a Habit We Should Break," *Guardian*, March 8, 2014, https://www.theguardian.com/commentisfree/2014/mar/08/americans-job-uncertainty-looking-for-new-life-meaning.

14. *The Office*, season 5, episode 5, "Employee Transfer," directed by David Rogers, aired October 30, 2008, on NBC, https://www.imdb.com/title/tt1248749.

15. Sarah L. Sanderson, *The Place We Make: Breaking the Legacy of Legalized Hate* (WaterBrook, 2023).

16. Sarah Sanderson, email message to author, March 10, 2024. Shared with permission.

17. George Herbert, "The Collar," in *Norton Anthology of English Literature: The Major Authors*, ed. Stephen Greenblatt, 9th ed. (Norton, 2013), 735–36.

18. Oswald Chambers, "The Voice of the Nature of God," *My Utmost for His Highest*, Our Daily Bread Ministries, January 16, 2024, https://utmost.org/classic/the-voice-of-the-nature-of-god-classic.

19. George Eliot, *Middlemarch* (Penguin Classics, 1988), 107–8.

20. Frederick Buechner, *Wishful Thinking: A Seeker's ABC* (HarperSanFrancisco, 1993), 119.

21. Garry Friesen, *Decision Making and the Will of God*, with J. Robin Maxson (Multnomah, 1980), 339.

22. Veith, *God at Work*, 23.

23. Veith, *God at Work*, 47.

24. Gordon T. Smith, *Courage and Calling: Embracing Your God-Given Potential*, rev. ed. (IVP Books, 2011), 65–68.

25. Kennedy, *One in a Millennial*, 247.

26. Guinness, *The Call*, 188.

27. Smith, *Courage and Calling*, 75.

The Transcendentals

1. Note that Paul's encouragement here does not mean we ought to exist as Pollyanna, shielding ourselves from harsh realities to live in a sugar-coated world seen through rose-colored glasses. To do so would mean ignoring the true. Truth is one of the transcendentals we will explore in the next chapter.

2. Jacques Maritain, *"Art and Scholasticism" with Other Essays* (Filiquarian, 2007), 35–36.

3. E. Lily Yu, *Break, Blow, Burn, and Make: A Writer's Thoughts on Creation* (Worthy, 2024), 96–98.

The True

1. It's a lot more complicated than I have space to address here, but the larger point is that Christians who care about truth neglected beauty to truth's peril, as well as beauty's.

2. John-Mark L. Miravalle, *Beauty: What It Is and Why It Matters* (Sophia Institute, 2019), 42.

3. Miravalle, *Beauty*, 42.

4. John 8:32; 3 John 4; Eph. 6:14; John 1:14; 16:13; 1:1–5; 14:6.

5. "Science (n.)," *Online Etymology Dictionary*, updated October 16, 2022, https://www.etymonline.com/word/science.

6. Jordan B. Cooper, *In Defense of the True, the Good, and the Beautiful* (Just & Sinner, 2021), 19.

7. Viktor E. Frankl, *Man's Search for Meaning* (1946; repr., Beacon, 2006), 99.

8. Frankl, *Man's Search for Meaning*, 98.

9. "Logos," PBS, accessed August 21, 2024, https://www.pbs.org/faith andreason/theogloss/logos-body.html.

10. Emily Dickinson, "Tell All the Truth but Tell It Slant," in *The Complete Poems of Emily Dickinson*, ed. Thomas H. Johnson (Back Bay, 1961), 506–7.

11. Jon Collins and Tim Mackie, hosts, *How to Read the Bible*, podcast, episode 32, "The Tree of Knowing Good and Bad," BibleProject, June 17, 2019, https://bibleproject.com/podcast/tree-knowing-good-bad.

12. Robert W. Pazmiño and Octavio J. Esqueda, *Anointed Teaching: Partnership with the Holy Spirit* (Publicaciones Kerigma, 2019), 89.

13. Arthur Miller, *Death of a Salesman*, in *The Portable Arthur Miller*, ed. Christopher Bigsby (Penguin, 1997), 40.

14. Miller, *Death of a Salesman*, 129–30.

15. Os Guinness, *The Call: Finding and Fulfilling God's Purpose for Your Life*, 20th anniv. ed. (W, 2018), 177.

16. Kathleen A. Cahalan, *The Stories We Live: Finding God's Calling All Around Us* (Eerdmans, 2017), 25.

17. Dorothy L. Sayers, *Why Work?* (CreateSpace, 2014), 18.

The Good

1. William Dyrness, *Visual Faith: Art, Theology, and Worship in Dialogue* (Baker Academic, 2001), 70–74.

2. Gerard Manley Hopkins, "God's Grandeur," in *Gerard Manley Hopkins: Poems and Prose* (Penguin Classics, 1985), available at https://www.poetryfoundation.org/poems/44395/gods-grandeur.

3. Paul Buckley, "Matter and Its Creator," in *Why We Create: Reflections on the Creator, the Creation, and Creating*, ed. Jane Clark Scharl and Brian Brown (Square Halo, 2023), 22.

4. Diane Langberg, interview by Cherie Harder, Trinity Forum, July 9, 2021, available at https://youtu.be/XGT3AXDBLbA, transcript at https://www.ttf.org/portfolios/online-conversation-diane-langberg.

5. Cal Newport, *So Good They Can't Ignore You: Why Skills Trump Passion in the Quest for Work You Love* (Little, Brown, 2012), 38.

6. Newport, *So Good They Can't Ignore You*, 229.

7. Wendell Berry, "Christianity and the Survival of Creation," *Cross Currents* 43, no. 2 (Summer 1993), available at https://www.ecofaithrecovery.org/wp-content/uploads/2012/09/BerryWendell_ChristianitySurvivalCreation.pdf.

8. Dorothy L. Sayers, *Why Work?* (CreateSpace, 2014), 10.

9. Sayers, *Why Work?*, 11.

10. Sayers, *Why Work?*, 18, 19.

11. Sayers, *Why Work?*, 22.

12. Sayers, *Why Work?*, 20.

13. Garry Friesen, *Decision Making and the Will of God*, with J. Robin Maxson (Multnomah, 1980), 252.

14. Friesen, *Decision Making and the Will of God*, 336.

15. Newport, *So Good They Can't Ignore You*, 206.

16. Gene Edward Veith, *God at Work: Your Christian Vocation in All of Life* (Crossway, 2002), 152.

17. Cal Newport, *Deep Work: Rules for Focused Success in a Distracted World* (Grand Central, 2016), 90–91.

18. Gordon T. Smith, *Courage and Calling: Embracing Your God-Given Potential*, rev. ed. (IVP Books, 2011), 140.

19. Katie Andraski, Facebook direct message to author, June 28, 2024.

20. François-Marie Arouet de Voltaire, *Candide, or Optimism*, in *The Norton Anthology of World Masterpieces*, trans. Robert M. Adams, 7th ed. (Norton, 1999), 2:379.

21. Wendell Berry, "A Vision," from "To Think of the Life of a Man," in *The Selected Poems of Wendell Berry* (Counterpoint, 1998), 102. I recently encountered this poem in Lore Ferguson Wilbert's book, *The Understory: An Invitation to Rootedness and Resilience from the Forest Floor* (Brazos, 2024), xi–xii. I don't often remember where I first encountered a work, but in this case, it was both recent and memorable. Lore's book is beautiful, and when I opened it up and encountered this poem at its start, I was moved to tears. It was while I was drafting this book, so the poem landed at just the right time and in the right way.

The Beautiful

1. Thomas Aquinas, *Summa Theologiae*, part 1, question 5, article 1, https://www.newadvent.org/summa/1005.htm.

2. *Barbie*, directed by Greta Gerwig (Warner Bros., 2023).

3. For more on how aesthetic experience cultivates orthodoxy, orthopraxy, and orthopathy, see Lanta Davis, *Becoming by Beholding: The Power of the Imagination in Spiritual Formation* (Baker Academic, 2024), part 3.

4. Elaine Scarry, *On Beauty and Being Just* (Princeton University Press, 1999), 31.

5. Roger Scruton, *Beauty* (Oxford University Press, 2009), 15.

6. James K. A. Smith, *You Are What You Love: The Spiritual Power of Habit* (Brazos, 2016).

7. John-Mark L. Miravalle, *Beauty: What It Is and Why It Matters* (Sophia Institute, 2019), 15–16.

8. Miravalle, *Beauty*, 20.

9. Miravalle, *Beauty*, 12.

10. John Mark Comer, *Garden City: Work, Rest, and the Art of Being Human* (Zondervan, 2015), 115.

11. "Beatitude (n.)," *Online Etymology Dictionary*, accessed August 21, 2024, https://www.etymonline.com/search?q=beatitude.

12. Thomas Aquinas, *Summa Theologiae*, part 1, question 39, article 8, https://www.newadvent.org/summa/1039.htm#article8.

13. Trinitarian principles are everywhere!

14. Gerard Manley Hopkins, "Pied Beauty," in *Gerard Manley Hopkins: Poems and Prose* (Penguin Classics, 1985), available at https://www.poetryfoundation.org/poems/44399/pied-beauty.

15. Iris Murdoch, *The Sovereignty of Good* (Routledge, 1971), 82.

16. Scarry, *On Beauty and Being Just*, 111–12.

17. Maggie Smith, "Poem Beginning with a Retweet," Blue Flower Arts, July 19, 2019, https://blueflowerarts.com/illuminations/poem-beginning-with-a-retweet.

18. Scarry, *On Beauty and Being Just*, 3.

19. Scarry, *On Beauty and Being Just*, 4–5.

20. Scarry, *On Beauty and Being Just*, 48.

21. Scruton, *Beauty*, 82.

22. Miravalle, *Beauty*, 35.

23. Scarry, *On Beauty and Being Just*, 93.

24. Scruton, *Beauty*, 82–91.

25. Scruton, *Beauty*, 82–96.

26. Walt Whitman, "I Hear America Singing," in *Selected Poems* (Dover, 1991), available at https://www.poetryfoundation.org/poems/46480/i-hear-america-singing.

Karen Swallow Prior (PhD, SUNY Buffalo) is the author of *The Evangelical Imagination: How Stories, Images, and Metaphors Created a Culture in Crisis*; *On Reading Well: Finding the Good Life Through Great Books*; *Fierce Convictions: The Extraordinary Life of Hannah More—Poet, Reformer, Abolitionist*; and *Booked: Literature in the Soul of Me*. She is coeditor of *Cultural Engagement: A Crash Course in Contemporary Issues* and has contributed to numerous other books. Prior is a frequent speaker, a senior fellow at the Trinity Forum, a contributing writer at *The Dispatch*, and a monthly columnist at Religion News Service.

Connect with Karen:

- @karenswallowprior
- @karenswallowprior
- The Priory (https://karenswallowprior.substack.com/)
- @KSPrior